{ Revised Edition }

a y e a r o f

Living
Mindfully

52
Quotes
Weekly &
Mindfulness
Practices

Richard Fields, Ph.D. – Editor, Co-author

Published by FACES Confer
Tucson, AZ
www.facescon*f*

This book is dedicated

to my mother, Libby Fields.

A note of gratitude for all our FACES Conferences speakers
(facesconferences.com) who contributed to our book.

I am grateful to Jack Kornfield and Tara Brach
for embracing the idea for this book.

A special thanks to our talented designer Don Stayner, www.dsdwerx.com
and our Art Director, Lisa Bradshaw, Ellebee Photography.

Thanks to Audrey Hall for designing the Revised Edition cover
and to Rachel Part for her help with this edition.

{ TABLE OF CONTENTS }

SECTION V ▪ **Important Mindfulness Practices**

SECTION VI ▪ **Being in Difficult Life Situations: Stress & Suffering**

Developing a Mindful Attitude

In 2007, I attended the UCLA Mindfulness & Psychotherapy conference, a conference that changed both my professional and personal life. Among the speakers who addressed our group were Zen Master Thich Nhat Hanh, Jack Kornfield, Ph.D., Daniel J. Siegel, M.D., and Tara Brach, Ph.D.

Jack Kornfield writes about this gathering in the opening pages of his book *The Wise Heart*:

"As I stood at the podium looking over a crowd of almost two thousand people, I wondered what had drawn so many to the three-day gathering. Was it the need to take a deep breath and find a wiser way to cope with the conflict, stress, fears, and exhaustion so common in modern life? Was it the longing for a psychology that included the spiritual dimension and the highest human potential in the vision of healing? Was it a hope to find simple ways to quiet the mind and open the heart?"

The answer: It was all of these things and more. On the last day of the conference, this group of counselors followed Thich Nhat Hanh on a silent walking meditation. One small step at a time, repeating to ourselves with each alternating step, "I have arrived.... I am home." Indeed, we were home in a community of healers with the common mission of incorporating mindfulness into our personal and professional lives. Our walk culminated in a silent lunch on the campus of UCLA that sunny Saturday.

It was at that point that I saw the many benefits of mindfulness, including its role in creating psychological well-being.

A Mindful Shift

For 25 years my company, FACES Conferences — Family and Addiction Conferences and Educational Seminars — had been providing continuing education training on psychiatric disorders and substance abuse to thousands of counselors, psychologists and social workers. In response to the UCLA conference, I shifted the FACES mission to integrate mindfulness, meditation and dharma (Buddhist teachings) into the counseling field.

Over the last five years, we have put on three to four mindfulness and counseling conferences annually, with attendance ranging from 300 to 850 counselors per day per conference. We have trained thousands of counselors in the application of mindfulness to their counseling practice, their personal lives and the lives of their clients.

This book is a way for the teachers at our FACES conference to bring mindfulness to you. It is fun, simple and easy to use.

A handbook of quotations, it outlines some very easy ways to practice mindfulness in everyday life. It will help you to adopt a mindful attitude, one that brings huge benefits to health, well-being, mind, body and soul.

Those who are beginners and do not have a meditation or mindfulness practice will benefit from this book, as will those who are experienced in mindfulness.

THE METHOD

I invited 30 of our FACES Conferences mindfulness teachers to pick their favorite mindfulness quotes and to answer the following questions:

Why did you choose this quote?
Why is this quote important when practicing mindfulness?
What are the mindfulness teaching points for this quote?
What are some suggested mindfulness practices for the week?

You'll find a photo and bio for each participating teacher in the appendices.

WHY 52 QUOTES?

We have 52 quotes so you have one quote a week to work with for each week of the year. And there are many precedents for this type of organization. The Buddha habitually numbered things – 4 Noble Truths, the 8-Fold Path, to use just a few examples.

QUOTE CATEGORIES

The quotes we received from our teachers, while all independent of each other, touched on several overlapping themes. They are organized into eight categories:

I   – *Developing Mindful Awareness*
II   – *Developing Mindful Attention*
III – *Being Present & In the Now*
IV   – *Having Compassion for Self & Others*
V   – *Important Mindfulness Practices*
VI   – *Being in Difficult Life Situations: Stress & Suffering*
VII – *Discovering Happiness & Joy*
VIII – *Interconnectedness & "Loving-kindness"*

Each section builds upon the previous section, so it is suggested you go in order.

HOW TO USE THE BOOK

This book is designed to help you focus on one mindfulness quote and practice per week. You can write down the quote and hang it up where you can read it regularly. This might mean your refrigerator — always a good place to be mindful — your office, on your computer, on your phone… someplace where you will see it frequently throughout the week. You might want to memorize the quote, or just keep it in your consciousness.

You can then follow the suggested mindfulness practice for the week for that quote. It is also suggested that during each week you keep a journal. One or more times a week, write down any observations, awareness, attentions, feelings, and intentions that come to you.

You might notice that you love certain quotes and find their associated practices enjoyable. You might also dislike certain quotes, and find them annoying or disturbing. Ironically, the quotes that cause displeasure may be the most important ones for you.

WHAT IS MINDFULNESS?

It's easy to lose ourselves in a barrage of rapidly flowing thought streams that flood our consciousness, creating a meandering current of distractions. Mindfulness has been described as awareness, attention, and remembering — remembering to remember to pay attention.

Compassion and interconnectedness are at the core of a mindful attitude.

Mindfulness is about being present and aware when dealing with both pleasant and unpleasant emotions and situations. We can learn to put these unpleasant feelings at arm's length and to not make them worse by being reactive and self-critical.

Most importantly, mindfulness is about having an open heart. It is the pivotal and essential element of mindfulness.

IS IT DIFFICULT TO HAVE A MINDFUL ATTITUDE?

Mindfulness is as simple as walking and talking — which are complex skills that take years to perfect, when you think about it. Much like any new skill, a regular mindfulness practice will grow and blossom as it becomes a regular part of your life.

The quotes in this book help you to remember to practice mindfulness in your everyday life. This book is designed to help you when you lose your way. You can pick it up, start rereading and get back to a mindful attitude.

Please join us on this heartfelt mission to bring mindfulness to your life and to those around you.

Section I

{ QUOTES Nº 1 TO 4 }

Developing Mindful Awareness

Mindfulness helps us to seek truth and develop awareness.
This, in turn, helps us to have more clarity and consciousness,
and to be more balanced, accepting and connected.

DANIEL J. SIEGEL, M.D., CHOSE THIS QUOTE:

"

You must be the change you wish to see in the world.

"

Mahatma Gandhi

This often-cited quotation is not usually offered as an example of mindfulness, but for me it serves as a powerful and succinct reminder of the essence of what mindfulness means. Mindfulness is certainly a state of awareness involving a set of qualities in the present moment in which we focus attention without being swept up by prejudgments. Some also place being kind and compassionate to ourselves as a part of the texture of this mindful state. *Mindfulness is also a set of traits described as a way of being that is imbued with being awake to what is happening as it is happening, of having emotional equanimity, of being able to sense the inner nature of our mental lives.*

In both mindful states and mindful traits, there is a way of being that we can strive for that brings internal balance and interpersonal connection. *The words from Mahatma Gandhi remind us that change begins with ourselves.* If we want to see kindness and compassion in the world, we must begin with kindness and compassion within ourselves. *If we want others to have clarity of focus, to be present for life as it unfolds, to be awake to the wondrous mysteries of this time we call our lives, then we must begin to cultivate these very qualities ourselves.*

Within these words, too, we see the two powerful aspects of all mindful awareness practices:

"Awareness of awareness,

and

attention to intention."

To be the change we wish to see in the world, we need to be aware of our awareness, to hold within this place of knowing our own unfolding sense of being awake. The notion of being the change "you wish to see in the world" also requires that we hold our own intention in the front of our minds — that we pay attention to our intention. In these many ways, Gandhi was offering to us a powerful sentiment at the heart of what it means to be mindful. Taken into our hearts and heads, our minds can bring mindfulness into the world from the inside out. Not bad for a dozen words!

The Wheel of Awareness

Let yourself get settled. It's good to sit with your back straight
if you can, feet planted flat on the floor, legs uncrossed.
If you need to lie flat on the floor that's okay, too.
And with your eyes open first, just try this.
Try letting your attention go to the center of the room.
Now just notice your attention as you let it go to the far wall.
And now follow your attention as it comes back to the middle
of the room and then up close as if you're holding a book
at reading distance. Notice how your attention
can go to very different places.

Now let your attention go inward. You might let your eyes
go closed, and as they go closed get a sense inside of you
of your body in space where you're sitting in the room.
And now let yourself become aware of the sounds around you.
That sense of sound can fill your awareness.
(Pause for some moments.)

Let your awareness now find the breath wherever
you feel it most prominently — whether it's at the level
of your nostrils, the air going in and out, or the level
of your chest as it goes up and down, or the level
of your abdomen going inward and outward.
Perhaps you'll notice your whole body breathing.
Wherever it comes naturally, just let your awareness
ride the wave of your in-breath, and then your out-breath.
(Pause.)

When you come to notice, as often happens,
that your mind may have wandered and become lost
in a thought or a memory, a feeling, a worry, when you
notice that, just gently, lovingly, return your awareness toward
the breath — wherever you feel it — and follow that
wave of the in-breath and the out-breath.
(Pause).

*As you follow your breath, I'm going to tell you an ancient story
that's been passed through the generations.*

*The mind is like the ocean. And deep in the ocean,
beneath the surface, it's calm and clear. And no matter what
the surface conditions are, whether flat or choppy or even
a full gale storm, deep in the ocean it's tranquil and serene.
From the depth of the ocean you can look toward the surface and
just notice the activity there, just as from the depth of the mind
you can look upward toward the waves, the brainwaves at the surface
of your mind, all that activity of mind—the thoughts, feelings,
sensations, and memories. Enjoy this opportunity
to just observe those activities at the surface of your mind.*

*At times it may be helpful to let your attention
go back to the breath, and follow the breath to ground you
in this deep tranquil place. From this depth of your mind,
it's possible to become aware of the activities of the mind
and to discern that those are not the totality of who you are:
That you are more than just your thought, more than just a feeling.
You can have those thoughts and feelings and also be able to just
notice them with the wisdom that they are not your identity.
They are simply one part of your mind's experience.
For some, naming the type of mental activity, like "feeling" or
"thinking," "remembering" or "worrying," can help allow these
activities of the mind to be noted as just mental events and
let them just gently float away and out of awareness.
(Pause.)*

The refuge of radiant
awareness is…
Closer than we can imagine.
More profound than
we can imagine.
Easier than we can imagine.
More wondrous than
we can imagine.

Jamgon Kongtrul the First, Tibetan Buddhist teaching

Awareness is the essence of what we are. While we can't visualize or describe this innate wakefulness, reflecting on these beautiful reassurances can turn us toward our true nature.

Closer than we can imagine. What if today, just right now, is all you have? Can you allow yourself to arrive in the center of now and experience the alert inner stillness within? Can you sense the consciousness that is looking through your eyes, listening to sounds, perceiving sensation? What is it like to recognize that awareness is closer than you can imagine?

More profound than we can imagine. Ask yourself, "Am I dreaming?" and look to see if your mind is occupied in a story of reality that is veiling the mystery. What happens if you stop for just a moment, step out of your thoughts, and sense the space between and around them? Can you let yourself rest in the space of not-knowing? Can you sense the measureless depth and wakefulness of inner space? What is it like to recognize that awareness is more profound than you can imagine?

Easier than we can imagine. The Sufi poet Hafiz says that we are different from the saints because we still think we have "a thousand serious moves." *But just as we fall asleep and get lost in doing, we can fall awake.* Invite yourself to be at ease, to give up any planning or attempts to control. Relax your body and mind, and allow everything to happen — sounds, sensations, feelings. Explore what it means to fall back into presence, to truly rest in presence. Can you sense the wakeful openness that is always and already here? What is it like to realize that coming home to awareness is easier than you can imagine?

More wondrous than we can imagine. Awareness experiences its own essence through the sensitivity of our body, heart and mind. Can you sense that, right now, awareness is experiencing its own dynamism, aliveness and creativity in your body? Can you sense that it is realizing its capacity for boundless love through your heart? Can you sense that it is awakening to its vastness and luminosity through your mind? What is it like to realize that living with this awakened body, mind, and heart is more wondrous than you can imagine?

Adapted from Brach, *True Refuge* (Random House, 2013)

{ MINDFULNESS PRACTICE FOR THE WEEK }

Take a few minutes to reflect on these four reminders.
Then as you move through your day, periodically pause and ask
yourself, "Is awareness here?" Notice what it is like to be aware
of your own awareness. In time, this formless luminous presence
will become more familiar as the truth of what you are than
any story you might have about yourself.

RICHARD FIELDS, Ph.D. CHOSE THIS QUOTE:

"

The essence of bravery is being without self-deception.

"

Pema Chodron

THEME – SELF-DECEPTION (DELUSION)

Self-deception is the opposite of awareness.
Denial is a way to avoid the fact that you might have a problem. It is a form of
self-delusion. Practicing to not deceive ourselves, with eyes and heart open,
invites awareness and self-discovery.

I worked for over thirty years in the field of alcohol/drug recovery and relapse
prevention. In counseling, in 12-step meetings, in everyday conversation we
often talk about denial of alcohol/drug dependence and relapse-prone
behaviors. A good way to remember the definition of denial is this acronym:

D – **D**on't

E – **E**ven

N – k**N**ow

I – **I**

A – **A**m

L – **L**ying.

You can remember this phrase and remind yourself to check if you are in "denial."

We all have self-deceptions and delusions, and how humbling it is when we
begin to awake from them. It is painful to see our own faults and mistakes.
It's so much easier to choose delusion over awareness.

There are common delusions about who we are in the world, as compared
with who we think we are. So you can see why Pema Chodron considers it a
brave act to be without self-deception (delusion).

─────{ MINDFULNESS PRACTICE FOR THE WEEK }─────

This week try to see things as they are. Ask yourself the question
"Am I lying to myself?" periodically throughout your day.
Ask further questions to clarify.

Try not to judge, but instead accept.
Explore whether you might be hiding from some truth
or fear that may be painful and cause suffering.

STEVEN HAYES, Ph.D. CHOSE THIS QUOTE:

Because in much wisdom there is much grief, and increasing knowledge results in increasing pain.

Ecclesiastes 1:18

Mindfulness training should come with a warning. This path is not about hanging on to good feelings, although good feelings may come. It is about cultivating an open, loving connection to oneself and others. There is no way to do that without touching pain, and not just that, but learning to carry it as a universal, much as we carry gravity or breathe air.

When we bring open awareness to ourselves, we inevitably see our own dark and difficult places and begin to realize that the natural tendency of the human mind is to try to sort experiences into the ones we want or do not want. This is not a wise guide. Grasping for feelings called "good" requires that we stand aside from ourselves in judgment — an act that in and of itself rips and tears at the wholeness of awareness.

A while ago, I made a quick trip to the grocery store. As I got out of my car, I was stopped in my tracks by the sight of an old woman struggling to pull her shopping cart from an outside stall. Finally successful, she directed it toward the door, draping her large, thick limbs over it as if she might otherwise fall down. Bent at the waist, she slowly forced one foot forward, and then another, almost unable to lift her heavy legs. As I was watching this unfold I could feel the painful effort she was exerting. Tears began to come to my eyes and, oddly, a bittersweet smile formed on my face. I'm not sure I can say why, except that there was nobility and a sense of humanness in her struggle.

Suddenly she turned her head in my direction. Her eyes touched mine, and held my gaze for a moment. There was a sense of time slowing down and space changing, as if she was just inches away. A kind smile came over her face. I saw her seeing me, seeing her. I don't think her smile was an attempt to rescue me; it felt more like an acknowledgement of shared awareness. She knew that I knew this was hard and she let me know we were together in consciousness.

In that moment, she was not just "an old woman hunched over her shopping cart." In a deep sense she was me, and I was her. Her pain was my pain. I'm not certain, but I think she knew that. As she turned back to her painful task of walking into the store, a part of me walked with her.

You cannot cut off the expansion of human consciousness without doing violence to its essence.

There is no way to open up fully to our own experiences, our joys and sorrows, without opening to the joy and pain of others, at other times, and in other places. The suffering and satisfactions of anyone, anywhere, anytime is in some way ours, now. The children who have too little to eat are with us. The wars that are being fought are with us. The injustices being done visit us now.

When we touch human consciousness in a full and open way, we move beyond the content of awareness to the vessel of consciousness that contains that content. Suffering happens when we leave this vessel and become too invested in the content it contains. With wisdom, we learn how to be who we are, and we see that this vessel is far larger than the teacup defined by our own body. It is as large as consciousness itself, boundless, timeless. It transforms suffering but it does not eliminate pain. Not if you go to the grocery store.

1. *Using whatever practice you commonly use, as you sit in open non judgmental awareness of your own sensations, thoughts and emotions, expand your awareness to include the room you are in, without subtracting from your contact with experiences within the skin.*

2. *Move your point of awareness to another part of the room and become aware of yourself sitting where you were sitting, as if looking back at yourself. Allow yourself to experience the room itself from this different perspective, while continuing to hold your experiences compassionately, lovingly, and openly. If new experiences emerge as you see yourself from a different spatial perspective, note these. Then return to step 1.*

3. *Move your point of awareness to a distant, wiser future, and become aware of yourself sitting where you are sitting, as if looking back at yourself through time. Continue to hold your experiences compassionately, lovingly and openly. If new experiences emerge as you see yourself from a different temporal perspective, note these. Then return to step 1.*

4. *Picture a person you know well and picture a time you were in the presence of that person. It does not matter initially if the moment was peaceful or conflicted; as you practice this skill you can choose different people or types of moments. Take the time to become aware of your own thoughts, feelings and bodily sensations and then expand your awareness to include what you sensed may have been the other person's thoughts, feelings and bodily sensations. Hold both sets in an open, compassionate, loving way. Now move your point of awareness inside the other person and imagine looking from behind his or her eyes back at yourself. Take the time to become aware of whatever thoughts, feelings and bodily sensations are inside this new body, and then expand your awareness to include the thoughts, feelings, and bodily sensations of the person you are looking at: "yourself." Hold both sets in an open, compassionate, loving way. Then return to step 1.*

Practice step 2 and 3 for brief moments throughout the day, becoming aware of your own experiences from different perspectives defined by space and time.

*Practice step 4 for brief moments throughout the day with people you meet, people you read about or people you see on television and computer screens. **As an act of compassion, love and connection, take just a second to hold their joys and sorrows in open awareness. Hold the pain of others as if it were your own. In some deep sense, it is.***

Section II

{ QUOTES № 5 TO 8 }

Developing Mindful Attention

Mindful attention helps us embrace creativity
and possibility while quieting reactivity.

GREGG KRECH CHOSE THIS QUOTE:

Sometimes I go about in pity for myself, and all the while a great wind is bearing me across the sky.

Ojibwa saying

More than 20 years ago, I had an epiphany while hiking in the Blue Ridge Mountains on a cool, spring day. I was trying to reach a ridge that overlooked the Shenandoah Valley, but a combination of heavy winds and spring storms had toppled many trees and large limbs, which blocked the trail. I found myself getting more and more irritated as I ascended. Rather than enjoying my hike, I was mentally lamenting the lack of trail maintenance. I found myself frustrated by all the little detours and climbs I had to make to get around the trail's obstacles.

On my way down, I decided to do some research by counting both the number of trees and limbs that were in the way and also the number of those that had been removed or moved aside. The latter were harder to spot because I had to scan the sides of the trail for the cut ends of logs or for limbs that had been pushed aside. To my astonishment, *there were more trees and limbs that had been moved than those that were in the way!* Yet while hiking up this same trail, my experience had been one of frustration because I had kept my attention only on the obstacles that were in the way. At that point, I came to a realization: *"Your experience of life is not based on your life, but on what you pay attention to."*

This same idea is represented in the Ojibwa saying, which we keep posted in the hallway during our retreats. There is a great web of care and support that allows us to live our life each day. Even in the first hour of the day, the list of how we are supported is extensive — showers, hot water, a towel, soap, coffee, a toothbrush, toothpaste, breathable air, appliances, socks, etc… These are all manifestations of the "wind" that the Ojibwa refer to. And each of these manifestations has karmic depth. The hot water is heated by a hot water heater, which was installed and delivered by two people who work for the company that sold it. The water travels through pipes that were installed by a plumber when the house was built. Those pipes are made of copper which was mined in Montana. So while we are being carried by this compassionate wind, where is our attention? Too often it is caught up in thoughts of self-pity: Why is my life so hard? Why didn't I sleep better? Why doesn't my spouse appreciate me more instead of criticizing me? Why is life overwhelming me with so much to do?

When our attention gets trapped by the obstacles in life, we lose sight of the wind. Of course, the wind is there whether we notice it or not. But our experience of life — the past day, or the past year — is based on what we're paying attention to. *The Japanese method of self-reflection known as Naikan is designed to help us shift our attention in a more constructive direction, so we don't forget about the wind.* But our initial work is to learn to be aware of our attention. Our ability to shift our attention determines our ability to change our experience. *Most of us spend a great deal of effort trying to improve our circumstances. But we spend very little effort trying to improve our attention skills — which determine our experience.*

*This practice requires that you set aside
20 minutes for quiet self-reflection.*

■

*Select a difficult situation you faced at some point in the past.
It can be a health problem, a divorce or separation, a tragedy
that caused damage to your home like a fire or hurricane.
Perhaps you were laid off from your job or had financial problems.*

■

*Select a time frame to examine — no more than a
three-month period during which you had this difficulty.*

■

*Take a sheet of paper and divide it into two columns.
Label the left column with a title that characterizes
the difficult situation you have selected. Label the right column
"Support/Care Received in Other Areas."*

■

*Spend the first 10 minutes listing the support and care
you received in relation to your difficult situation.*

■

*Spend the next 10 minutes reflecting on the support
you received during the same time in other areas of your life.*

■

*At the end of your period of self-reflection you should
have two detailed lists of the support and care
you've received during that period of time.
This is the "great wind bearing you across the sky."*

KRISTIN NEFF, Ph.D., CHOSE THIS QUOTE:

When one door of happiness closes, another opens, but often we look so long at the closed door that we do not see the one that has been opened for us.

Helen Keller, We Bereaved, *1929*

This quote deeply humbles me. A woman who was both blind and deaf, Helen Keller changed the world because of — not in spite of — her disabilities.

Life is in a constant state of flux and change. This means that we will inevitably lose things we dearly love, whether they are people, objects, or hopes and dreams. *It also means that we will gain the unexpected, and that we will be presented with undreamed of opportunities for love, growth, and discovery.*

When we only focus on what we have lost, however, or what we want but don't have, we often don't notice these opportunities. We miss what is right beneath our noses. But there is a silver lining to almost every cloud, a truth to which most people can attest.

{ MINDFULNESS PRACTICE FOR THE WEEK }

Here's a practice that can help you see possibilities and not just problems in life. First, think of one or two of the biggest challenges you've faced in your life so far, problems that were so difficult you thought you'd never get through them at the time. In hindsight, can you see if anything good came out of the experience? Did you grow as a person, learn something important, find more meaning in your life, develop a new relationship? If you could, would you go back in time and change what happened if it meant that you wouldn't be the person you are now because of it?

Now think about a challenge you're facing right now. Are there any positive things that might come out of your present circumstances — any learning opportunities, career possibilities, new relationships, ways to re-organize your priorities? **What is life trying to teach you right now?** *Is there any way that this seeming curse might actually be a gateway to a beautiful new adventure?*

For the next week, try to intentionally reframe any difficult or challenging experiences in this way, and see what happens!

RONALD D. SIEGEL, PSY.D. CHOSE THIS QUOTE:

66

What you resist, persists.

99

Attributed to Carl Jung

THEME – ATTENTION TOWARD WHAT ARISES

Of all the mechanisms of the mind revealed through mindfulness practice, resistance may cause the most grief. It plays a central role in my own suffering and in most of the problems that prompt people to seek counseling.

Some examples are obvious: Who hasn't noticed that trying to fall asleep can cause sleepless nights, trying to stay calm can make us agitated and trying to maintain sexual arousal is the fastest way to lose it? And who doesn't know people who drink to feel better, only to wind up feeling worse; *or who constrict their lives out of fear, only to grow more fearful?*

Other examples are a bit more subtle: The pious person who eschews sexual feelings only to be plagued by them, the kind person who denies angry feelings only to have them emerge as mysterious bodily pains or passive-aggressive behavior, or the tough, masculine guy who feels compelled to attack split-off aspects of himself that he sees in more sensitive types.

All of these maladies involve experiential avoidance — trying to make uncomfortable feelings, sensations or thoughts go away.

It's a strategy that almost all of us try, but it never works for long, and it usually backfires, for when we bury feelings, we bury them alive.

Mindfulness practice offers an alternative. *By turning our attention toward whatever arises in consciousness, whether pleasurable or painful, and trying to open fully to our experience, we enable the mind to operate with greater ease.* We notice that no feeling, thought or sensation lasts indefinitely. We also stop accumulating disavowed, split-off feelings that cause anxiety by threatening to flood into consciousness the moment we slow down. *By opening ourselves up to pleasure and pain, we're not plagued by so many symptoms.*

Another benefit of embracing our experience is that it leads to compassion toward ourselves and other, for whatever pain or evil we see in other people we've already seen and accepted in our own heart and mind. The world is no longer populated by good and bad people, us and them, but only by struggling fellow beings.

{ MINDFULNESS PRACTICE FOR THE WEEK }

EMBRACING EXPERIENCE

When we find ourselves wishing our mind would be other than it is, pushing away or distracting ourselves from something uncomfortable, we can simply ask, "What am I resisting here?" It often helps to close our eyes and bring attention to sensations in the body — to notice where there's tightness, constriction or perhaps the hint of an emotion. We can then breathe into these sensations and ask ourselves, "What might this be?" Sometimes an image or thought will come to mind that illuminates the resistance, letting us see what we're having difficulty accepting. **True to the principal that "what we resist, persists," a gentle balance is needed, so we practice accepting our resistance as we begin to let it go.**

{ 8 }

"

Wander into the center of the circle of wonder.

"

Hongzhi Zhengjue

THEME – WANDER & WONDER

The 12th-century Chinese Chan Zen teacher Hongzhi Zhengjue encourages us to "wander into the center of the circle of wonder." This is his way of describing what "just sitting" feels like. *The mind, which naturally wanders, can be tamed by the practice of attentional training. But once it has learned to be still, it is free to do what it loves to do. Thoughts still occur, emotions pass through the body/mind, sensations come and go, but we don't get caught in any of this passing experience.* We understand that the nature of the mind is to wander. In this wandering, everything that is encountered is a teaching, a pointing to a life that can be vividly lived. And every path we wander leads to the same place: "Here". *The realization of the continual return to this moment, this time, this place is liberating. A sense of wonder arises, of not knowing, and deeply trusting this feeling of simple presence.*

*You can use this quote often to remind yourself to
loosen up your opinions about what you think
you're doing or where you think you're going.*
This is a practice that can be done informally,
with regular reminders to yourself throughout the day.
Or you can do a formal wandering practice.
Sitting in an upright posture, allow yourself
to be with your breath, your body and all of your
sense perceptions, thoughts and emotions.
You can notice how all of these experiences
come and go, as long as you don't try
to hold on to any one of them. This is a practice of release
from effort, and allows a sense of peace and not knowing
to arise naturally. If you have spent most of your
time and energy training your mind to focus,
you may want to give yourself this gift of wandering.
"Wander into the center of the circle of wonder."
Enjoy your life.

Section III

Being Present
& In the Now

*We can choose to be present for the pleasure and the pain,
the comfort and discomfort, the good mood and the bad mood.
We can also awaken and be present in nature and the cycle of life.
We can be more present in each moment, and to make the best
decision in that moment of living. Remember to focus on your
breath, meditation practice, and pausing as well.*

ELISHA GOLDSTEIN, Ph.D. CHOSE THIS QUOTE:

"

Wherever you are, that is the entry point.

"

Kabir, 15th-century Indian poet

The mental health benefits of a mindfulness practice are well established. Cultivating a more mindful life isn't often easy, however. There are many obstacles at play. I love to bring up this quote by the 15th-century Indian poet Kabir again and again because it gets underneath these obstacles and drops us into mindfulness.

This is the underlying truth behind mindfulness. If the intention is to bring awareness to the direct experience of the present moment with fresh eyes, then life itself becomes the practice.

What's so powerful about understanding that "wherever you are, that is the entry point" is that it frees us of this false belief that we need to be in a certain head space to train our minds toward mindfulness. *Even feelings of doubt, agitation, restlessness and boredom are the entry points to the present moment.*

What if we changed the way we saw these uncomfortable feelings that drive us away from our intentions? What if instead of trying to get away from them we saw them as parts of ourselves that are anchors to the present moment? *They are entry points into a space of choice, possibility, opportunity and freedom. This is "The Now Effect".*

When we use uncomfortable feelings as entry points, we also send the message internally that we are worthy of attention. One thing we know from learning theory is that we get more of whatever we practice and repeat in life. The more we turn away from ourselves in difficult moments, the more we water the ideas in our mind that we're not worth paying attention to. In other words, we are watering the seeds of unworthiness.

{ MINDFULNESS PRACTICE FOR THE WEEK }

*What can you do to **remember that no matter what is happening in your life at any given moment, that it can be used in the practice of mindfulness?***

Maybe it would help to write down the quote and put it up at work or at home. Perhaps use it as the background on your phone; we all know how often we look at those nowadays. Or maybe try to stay connected through a local or online community that reminds you of these important mindful lessons.

Be intentional right now and consider a way to create that 180-degree shift and change what drives you away from the present moments of your life into supports that remind you to be present.

MICHAEL MEADE, D.H.L. CHOSE THIS QUOTE

66

In the beginner's mind there are many possibilities, in the expert's mind there are few.

99

Shunryu Suzuki

THEME – BEGINNER'S MIND – SHOSHIN

Becoming more mindful at a meaningful level can result in a greater capacity for openness to both inner and outer experiences, as described in the Zen practice of *shoshin or beginner's mind*. Taking the attitude of a beginner makes us less subject to preconceived ideas and less restricted by preformed judgments. Being ready to begin anew diminishes automatic reactions based upon old patterns of behavior. Whether an event appears surprising, threatening or tragic, it can be experienced with a fresh mind.

As the quote from Zen teacher Suzuki suggests, the expert may have dogmatic certainty, but the openness of the beginner is more likely to find the true nature of a situation. *Expert* comes from experience, yet no amount of experience can add up to wisdom. *Wisdom requires a willingness to learn and even a capacity to be foolish in the right direction.* Shoshin begins where common experience and accepted procedures leave off. It offers a particular kind of mindfulness, a wisdom practice based on a willingness to sit or walk or even dance at the edge where life remains open to many possibilities and as yet unseen potentials.

Like most enduring words, *shoshin* has more than one meaning. The same word that designates the practice of *beginner's mind can also mean correct truth*. When used in that sense, it denotes "a genuine signature on a work of art" or refers "to an item or person that is genuine." Thus, the practice of beginner's mind also involves the sense of originality that makes art compelling, as well as the authenticity that makes a person unique and valuable. Here, there seems to be a surprising ground, an open area where Eastern philosophies can encounter and exchange with Western ideas.

{ Mindfulness Practice for the Week }

Track the subtle ways that eternity tries to visit you,
whether it be through silent meditation or ecstatic dance.
Instead of being busy find more openings to timelessness.
Find at least one moment of eternity in each day;
refuse to go to sleep until you do so.

Choose a book of poems from a poet like Rumi,
Hafiz or Rilke or an author of similar imagination and courage.
Make sure the writer is capable of surprise like
the Zen rascal Ikkyu who wrote:

"If you break open the cherry tree,
Where are the flowers?
But in the springtime, see how they bloom!"

You want to sit at the feet of the words and be there
when the blooming happens. You want the randomly
chosen words to carry you to where the beginnings
endlessly blossom and your beginner's mind opens again
like the timeless lotus on the ancient pond.

JOHN BRIERE, Ph.D. CHOSE THIS QUOTE:

Thus shall ye think of all this fleeting world: A star at dawn, a bubble in a stream; A flash of lightning in a summer cloud; A flickering lamp, a phantom, and a dream.

Diamond Sutra

THEME – IMPERMANENCE AND THE HERE AND NOW

These are the last four lines of the Diamond Sutra. Aren't they beautiful?

Who can hang onto a star or a bubble? Like an orchid in your meditation area, these lines suggest that impermanence is not about absence, or even loss, but instead about the beauty implicit in ephemeral things – which, luckily enough, is everything.

Mindfulness, when fully engaged, allows us to inhabit the here and now, where stars emerge, bubbles burst and flashes of lightning come and go. None of these things last, nor do we. Trying to make it not so, hanging on to moments beyond their shelf lives — in fact, turning them into phantoms or dreams — leads to a special type of suffering. When I was a kid, this would happen when I would catch a butterfly, but then inadvertently kill it by "keeping" it in a jar. I loved it! Why did it die?

As an adult, I hang on to myself and loved ones, my personal history, my iPhone and really good take-out. And the occasional Chardonnay. And, OK, other stuff too. There's nothing intrinsically wrong with that, except that it means I have a lot to lose, and losing brings pain. And there's nothing wrong with pain, except that it can mutate into ongoing suffering when its source is an attachment to how things are supposed to be, rather than an acceptance of how they really are. *The Diamond Sutra counsels us to let the butterfly go, to let ourselves love and need, but to do so without a tight grasp or any expectations of durability.*

This is the gift of mindfulness. The here and now, when allowed to be so, contains reality and beauty. The orchid is beautiful when blooming, beautiful when dropping its petals, beautiful when a naked stem and beautiful when compost. *It's only when we try to keep it in full flower that we kill it in our minds.* Nothing wrong with that, either, I guess. Except that we miss a lot, and feel bad when we don't have to.

———————————{ MINDFULNESS PRACTICE FOR THE WEEK }———————————

The world around us is an ongoing meditation on arising and falling away, on the impermanence of all things. We suffer when we try to keep this natural cycle from unfolding, as it inevitably will.

This week, see if you can notice the constant coming and going, shifting and changing, of things around you without trying to evaluate or alter them. The sound of a car alarm, a homeless guy yelling at you, the smell of coffee, someone crying, a bird flitting by, a worry. **Mindfulness in this context means that you "just" experience these things, letting them happen without judging them, without making them stay or go. Is it possible to experience this flash of lightning, that butterfly, without jarring them up?** *Sometimes when this happens, joy emerges from circumstances that otherwise might go unappreciated. This meditation needs no cushion. It can happen anywhere, at any time.*

TARA BRACH, Ph.D. CHOSE THIS QUOTE:

"

Between stimulus and response there is a space, and in that space lies our power and our freedom.

"

Viktor Frankl, Man's Search for Meaning, *1997*

THEME – A SACRED PAUSE: PRESENCE

We spend many of our moments in a trance. Rather than living from a wakeful presence, we tumble into the future, reacting to the changing array of pleasant and unpleasant experiences. The patterns of our reactivity form a limiting prison — they keep us from the creativity, aliveness and love that express our natural being.

The liberating practice of mindfulness begins with a pause. In that pause, we begin to notice what's happening — a worried thought, a flash of irritation, a craving for sweets. *With that recognition, we allow what is there to be there, without doing anything. I call this a* sacred pause: *In these moments of recognizing and allowing life to be just as it is, we enter the space of freedom.* You might try it now. Just stop for a moment, feel what is right here and simply be.

With practice, mindfulness reveals who we are beyond the limiting story of a separate self. Historic patterns of defensiveness and aggression loosen, and the light of our being shines through. As we inhabit this timeless presence, we naturally respond to the world with intelligence and care, with wonder and joy. *Our lives have power and beauty because we are living from the source.*

———————{ MINDFULNESS PRACTICE FOR THE WEEK }———————

FINDING THE SPACE OF FREEDOM

At a time when you feel calm, identify and write down several situations where you become moderately reactive — perhaps with anxiety or irritation. Some examples: "Getting my son ready for school," "being caught in rush hour traffic," "approaching a deadline for a project," "feeling fatigued at work," "being criticized by my partner."

Select one, and for the next week have the intention to pause inwardly in the midst of this situation. You might outwardly be moving, but discontinue any conversation and step out of your thoughts.

In the moment of pausing, the most important thing is to offer a non-judging, friendly quality of attention to your experience.
In fact, the friendlier the better! Honor that this is a moment of awakening and, in that spirit, take a real interest in what is happening inside you. Is there tension in your chest? Knots in your stomach? Numbness? Pressure? Are you aware of anger? Anxiety? Craving? What are you believing? Breathe with whatever sensations or emotions are there, and just offer them a respectful, allowing presence.

Depending on your situation, this step of pausing and attending to your feelings might take 30 seconds to a minute. Then take a few full breaths, relaxing with each out-breath, and resume your daily activity. Notice the difference between being caught in reactivity, and being awake, here and now.

RUBIN NAIMAN, Ph.D. CHOSE THIS QUOTE

"

Life is lived in the pauses, not the events.

"

Hugh Prather, Morning Notes: 365 Meditations to Wake You Up, *2005*

This quote not only satisfies my intellectual sensibilities, it actually inspires me to pause for a moment. It instantly calls me back to that place of stillness that hovers shyly behind the compelling visible layer of life.

Prather calls our attention to the common presumption that life is lived in the sequence of daily events — in the actions we take, the words we speak and the things we produce. *In a world where we're taught to seek meaning through such activities, it's refreshing to discover a gracious undercurrent of serenity in the still life spaces between events.*

We usually experience consciousness through awareness of the stream of events. In pausing, our awareness is withdrawn from this incessant flow and turns inward. Here, we can experience consciousness independently of events—what has been called pure consciousness. *In the pause, we experience who we really are beneath our awareness of events. We experience a deeper, more peaceful aspect of ourselves.*

In nine simple words, Prather also reminds us of a fundamental choice we are presented with every moment. *Do I fixate exclusively on the ever-changing surface of life's events, or will I also take pause and notice the backdrop of peace?* I love this quote because it reminds us that, despite our usual inattentiveness to it, a modicum of peace is always at hand.

{ MINDFULNESS PRACTICE FOR THE WEEK }

A PRACTICE OF PAUSING

Meditation and other relaxation techniques provide opportunities to ritualize a practice of pausing. In this quote, we are reminded that mindfulness is much more than a meditation practice. It is a way of living. **The simple practice of pausing can help us carry mindfulness into the rest of our lives.**

Let yourself notice the pauses in the flow of everyday life events. **This is not about inattention to events; it is about tuning into the natural bubbles of stillness that permeate these events.** *For example, notice the point of stillness between your in- and out-breath or the moment of respite when you're trying to recall something.*

In addition to noticing such natural pauses, practice intentionally pausing. Pause at stop signs, pause in long lines, pause when you find yourself waiting for something. When you are able, close your eyes for a few seconds to pause the visual movie of events.

Larry Cammarata, Ph.D. chose this quote:

66

I have arrived.
I am home.

99

Thich Nhat Hanh

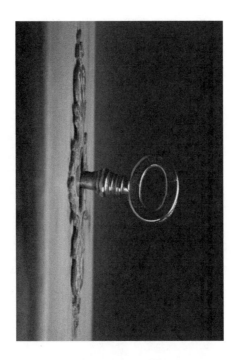

THEME – AT HOME

Hanging upon a wall in my bedroom, this verse by Zen Master Thich Nhat Hanh is penned in black calligraphy upon a beautifully framed piece of sky blue fabric.

"I have arrived. I am home," has become a welcoming friend to me. The depth of the message is supported by its simplicity, beauty and directness, a clear reflection of the teachings of its author.

This quote provides a gentle reminder that wherever we are, and whatever we are experiencing, we are always at home.

─┤ MINDFULNESS PRACTICE FOR THE WEEK ├─

Settle into your mindfulness practice by first silently connecting with the words "I have arrived" on the in-breath, and then connecting with "I am home" on the out-breath.

As another option, you can silently repeat, "Breathing in, I have arrived. Breathing out. I am home." Experiment with this centering exercise to make it your own. Welcome home!

Section IV

Having Compassion for Self & Others

Compassion and self-compassion are the foundation of all mindfulness practices. In Western culture we are prone to be hard on others, and even harder on ourselves.

This section offers you mindfulness practices to help with improving compassion for self and others.

15

Roshi Joan Halifax, Ph.D. chose this quote:

"

Love and compassion are necessities, not luxuries. Without them humanity cannot survive.

"

His Holiness the Dalai Lama

THEME – LOVE & COMPASSION

Compassion is a precious necessity for all of us. Here is a practice that you might find helpful in cultivating compassion in your life.

—————————{ MINDFULNESS PRACTICE FOR THE WEEK }——————————

First, find a quiet moment, a quiet space. Let your heart and mind settle. Then recall someone to whom you feel especially close, someone who you deeply wish to be free of suffering, whether the suffering is physical, social, mental or spiritual.

As you experience how this might feel, breathe deeply into your belly and track whatever you are sensing physically.

Recall that person's humanness and good qualities, as well as the suffering that he or she has been through or is going through.

Now internally repeat simple phrases of compassion toward the person you have visualized. With your breath, silently say to him or her:

"May you be free from this suffering...
May you be safe...
May you find peace."

Continue to visualize this person as you breath and silently say to him or her:

"May you be free from this suffering...
May you be safe...
May you find peace."

And for a final time, while visualizing your friend or relative silently and sincerely say to him or her:

"May you be free from this suffering...
May you be safe...
May you find peace."

Let your wish for this one person help strengthen your aspiration to help others.

16

SHAUNA L. SHAPIRO, Ph.D. CHOSE THIS QUOTE:

66

You can search throughout the entire universe for someone who is more deserving of your love and affection than you are yourself.

99

The Buddha

In this quote, *the Buddha offers the radical teaching that each of us is deserving of self-love.*

We are often taught that it is important to love thy neighbor as thyself. And yet, when we look closely at our own "self-love" we often find it is painfully lacking. Some years ago, one of my teachers invited me to reflect deeply on my relationship to myself. She asked, "Do you love yourself?" And when I reflected upon this, I was unsure. She suggested that I begin to say, "I love you, Shauna" each day and to try to feel and embody this. I looked at her as if she were crazy, and flat out said, "No, that's not the practice for me. It feels too forced and airy-fairy and I'm not sure it is authentic." She gently conceded, and offered a different practice, "How about simply saying, "Good Morning, Shauna."

"Yes" I replied, "that I can do." I had recently divorced and I would often wake up in the morning feeling sad and alone. Now, when I woke up, I began to say "Good morning, Shauna," and I felt the kindness and self-care in this simple morning greeting. After a few months, my teacher asked how the good morning practice was going. I shared how natural it had become and that I was actually enjoying it.

"It sounds like you have graduated," she responded with a soft smile. "Your next practice is to say, 'Good morning, I love you, Shauna.'" We both smiled. And the next morning I awoke and rotely said, "Good morning, I love you, Shauna." It felt a bit awkward. However, the patterning I had developed by simply saying "Good morning" allowed me to continue. Over the next weeks, I diligently greeted myself each day with "Good morning, I love you, Shauna."

And then, one morning, I felt "it." I actually felt love for myself pouring through me. Tears filled my eyes as I poignantly realized that I was experiencing self-love for the first time I could remember. I felt so vulnerable and raw. I also felt so grateful and so alive.

I would like to say that this feeling of self-love now pervades my every moment of lived experience, and that I float through life encapsulated in a soft white light of unconditional love. This is not the case. However, I can say that the pattern of self-love, once created, has never ceased to exist. It is something I can return to and remember over and over again. The American author and physician Oliver Wendell Holmes wrote that a "mind, once stretched... never regains its original dimensions." *I would add that a heart, once stretched, never regains its original dimensions.*

1. *Reflect upon the Buddha's teaching:*
"You can search throughout the entire universe
for someone who is more deserving of your love
and affection than you are yourself."
Do you believe this? What would it feel like
to let yourself believe this, just as an experiment?

2. *Each day when you wake up greet yourself with*
"Good Morning, [your name]." And if you are really brave,
try saying "Good morning, I love you [your name]."
I invite you to try saying this in different tones of voice,
softly, loudly, whispering it, silently… See what feels
most authentic and what most resonates in your body.
Play with it. Add movement or physical touch to the words.
I found that putting my hand over my heart when I greeted
myself significantly increased the felt sense of love.

3. *Share your experience with one dear friend,*
and invite them to do the practice with you.
Each morning you will say, "Good morning, I love you"
to yourselves and to each other.

(Adapted from the forthcoming book *Good Morning, I love you*, by Shauna L. Shapiro.)

KRISTIN NEFF, Ph.D. CHOSE THIS QUOTE:

Compulsive concern with 'I, me, and mine' isn't the same as loving ourselves... Loving ourselves points us to capacities of resilience, compassion, and understanding that are simply part of being alive.

Sharon Salzberg, The Force of Kindness, *2005*

THEME – ACCESSING NATURAL SELF-COMPASSION

I love this quote because it reminds us that self-compassion is actually a process of letting go. *When our hearts are open — when we allow ourselves to be touched by our own pain — we naturally respond with feelings of caring concern.* This isn't something we have to intentionally make happen. Rather, it is the very nature of the heart itself, a capacity merely to be uncovered rather than created anew. But what is it that's covering our hearts and preventing our love from flowing freely? The sense of a separate self.

When we see ourselves as distinct and cut off from others, we become obsessed with questions of who and what we are. Am I good or am I bad? Am I better than you or worse than you? Do I deserve compassion? Am I worthy of love?

When we recognize our shared and interconnected humanity, however, these concerns become irrelevant. Love is experienced in any moment of true connection — with others, with ourselves or with our moment-to-moment experience. Love is limitless because everything is connected, whether considered from the subatomic, cellular, psychological, social or global point of view. In order to know love, compassion and well-being, therefore, we only have to open our eyes to what's already here. *When we recognize our essential interconnectedness, we naturally find our resilient and boundless hearts.*

One way to access your natural self-compassion is to constantly remind yourself of your common humanity. When you find yourself lost in pain, self-criticism or feelings of unworthiness, try to remember that the human experience is imperfect – a reality we all share. Take a moment to consider how many countless others have had experiences so similar to your own. Rather than feeling isolated from others when you confront something in yourself or your life that you don't like, remember that nothing is wrong, abnormal or aberrant in imperfection. You are not alone. *By softening your sense of separate self in this way, your innate feelings of love and compassion will be able to emerge more freely.*

*One way to access your natural self-compassion
is to constantly remind yourself of your
common humanity. For the next week,
whenever you find yourself lost in pain,
self-criticism or feelings of unworthiness,
try to do two things:*

■

*Remember that the human experience is imperfect —
this is a reality we all share. Say something out loud
like "Imperfection is just part of life."*

■

*Take a moment to consider how many countless
others have had experiences so similar to your own.
Try to imagine all the diverse and varied ways
people have gone through just what
you're going through right now.*

■

*If you feel isolated from others when you confront
something in yourself or your life that you don't like,
try to remember that nothing is wrong, abnormal
or aberrant in imperfection. You are not alone.
By softening your sense of separate self in this way,
your innate feelings of love and compassion
will be able to emerge more freely.*

18

CHRIS GERMER, Ph.D. CHOSE THIS QUOTE:

We can still be crazy after all these years. We can still be angry after all these years. We can still be timid or jealous or full of feelings of unworthiness. The point is… not to try to throw ourselves away and become something better. It's about befriending who we are already.

Pema Chodron

THEME – SELF-COMPASSION

All human beings instinctively fight unpleasant experience at a very early, pre-conscious level. We fight ourselves when the experience is intense or disturbing enough. "What's wrong with me? Why me?" This is the unfortunate condition.

An alternative is self-compassion, a skill that can be learned by anyone. We can learn to give ourselves kindness and understanding not to feel better, *but* because *we feel bad.* It's a riddle, like a Zen koan. Can we respond to ourselves with compassion, naturally and spontaneously, just as we'd do for a beloved child? *Can we temporarily (and mercifully!) suspend our incessant striving to improve ourselves in order to care for ourselves?*

Imagine that your child has the flu and you know it will take about five days to work itself out of the body. Will you criticize the child for having the flu, expecting that your efforts will alleviate the illness, or will you soothe and comfort your child until the flu passes on its own? Self-compassion is just like that. *We don't need to add impatience to an already difficult situation.*

When we're dealing with an incurable physical illness, we might call in hospice for care and comfort after all other options have been exhausted. Ironically, in emotional life, *care* is *cure. When we stop beating ourselves up, a little space opens up around our problems and we can often see our way through.*

There are an infinite number of ways to cultivate self-compassion. Three key questions are:

What do I need now?
How do I care for myself already?
Can I give this to myself when I need it the most?

The problem is that the hard work of battling unpleasant experience is mostly a waste of time. Shortly before his death, Mark Twain said, "I am an old man and have known a great many troubles, but most of them never happened."

⎰ MINDFULNESS PRACTICE FOR THE WEEK ⎱

At its most basic level, self-compassion is intentional retraining. We're strengthening the wish to respond to suffering with warmth and kindness, replacing ill will with good will. Try repeating phrases during the day such as:

"May I be free from fear.
May I be free from shame.
May I be kind to myself.
May I be kind to others..."

In this way, we establish ourselves in basic kindness, for ourselves and then for others. Then, when we are under stress, we might find ourselves asking, "What do I need now?" and actually give it to ourselves, rather than living in constant threat mode and fighting meaningless battles throughout the day.

19

JOHN BRIERE, Ph.D. CHOSE THIS QUOTE:

66

Compassion is based on a keen awareness of the interdependence of all these living beings, which are all part of one another, and all involved in one another.

99

Thomas Merton, 1968

This quote isn't really Buddhist, per se. It's by Thomas Merton, a Trappist (Catholic) monk who lived from 1916 to 1968. He said these words in his last lecture, two hours before his death. Merton was a writer, poet and social activist who was powerfully affected by his contact with Zen Buddhism and by his interactions with the Dalai Lama, D.T. Suzuki and Thich Nhat Hanh, among others, in the 1950s and 1960s. So, it's sort of Buddhist.

What is compassion? *We can say that it is non judgmental awareness of the suffering of others, and ourselves, with the desire to relieve that suffering.* It is not a power position – it reflects our awareness that we are all traveling on the same bus, all of us subject to our histories and the events around us, doing what we can with the hand we've been dealt. So, when I sit with a distressed person, I don't want to feel pity (which implies superiority), but rather awareness that I, too, have difficult times -- in fact, but for luck, I might be where this person is at this particular moment. *My caring, then, includes shared experience. It doesn't elevate me, because we are both in the same situation, vulnerable to the inevitable impermanence of well-being.*

Compassion usually includes feelings of caring and warmth that are directed to someone regardless of his or her presumed lovability or positive traits. It is as relevant to the "bad" person as the "good" one. How we are in the world is a complex function of things like (but not limited to) genetics, child rearing, maltreatment by others, current relationships and the society in which we live – as well as the impacts of such factors on our perceptions and beliefs. Nobody does anything without reason. And if there are reasons, then understanding them will be more helpful than skipping them and forming an intrinsically limited (and limiting) judgment.

Buddhists call this dependent origination: the idea that all things arise from conditions and causes, which themselves arise from other causes and conditions. In other words, all events occur because of previous events. No event occurs independent of causality; everything arises (and falls away) as a function of innumerable other things that, themselves, arise and disappear.

So, what did Merton mean? I think he was saying that compassion requires awareness of dependent origination. *If we know that all of us are imbedded in a complex web of conditions, actions, and reactions, across time and interacting with one another on many levels, receiving and generating "causality" in vast loops of reciprocating influence, it is much harder to judge someone, or ourselves.*

*Start this week by taking a little time to sit by yourself.
Allow your mind to settle down. Do this in whatever way works for you.
If you are a meditator, meditate. If you are not, try focusing your mind
on your breath, notice yourself breathing in, breathing out.
Watch your thoughts come and go, without trying to control them.*

*When your mind is calm, think about someone you
know who is having a hard time or who is dealing with a
painful thing. It could be a friend, a loved one, someone
you don't like or maybe an animal you care about
(we'll call him or her a person, too. Why not?).
Bring his or her image to mind.*

*What do you want for this person? That he or she might suffer less,
that there could be some sense of peace in his or her life?
Importantly, even (perhaps especially) the "bad" person
is suffering, operating from his or her impacted beliefs
and expectations. Let yourself feel what your chosen person feels,
see what he or she sees. Try not to get lost in this person's
difficulty; watch it from the settled place that you have established.*

*Send caring feelings to this person. And to yourself, as someone
not that different from him or her, although perhaps more
fortunate at this point in time. Think about the things you
have in common, the things that you want that are the same.
Feel the connections between you.*

*Consider doing this exercise several times this week.
In between, try to notice the difficulties of others, moments when
they are less happy, stuck, in pain, frightened, angry, or sad.
Send them good wishes, too, and hopes that things will get
better for them. Note any gratitude that you might feel, living in
this complicated way, amid pain and happiness, never really alone.*

20

Shauna Shapiro, Ph.D. chose this quote:

> **The bud stands for all things,
> even for those things that don't flower,
> for everything flowers, from within,
> of self-blessing; though sometimes
> it is necessary to reteach a thing its
> loveliness, to put a hand on its brow of
> the flower and retell it in words and in
> touch it is lovely until it flowers again
> from within, of self-blessing...**

Galway Kinell, Saint Francis and the Sow, *1993*

THEME – RELEARNING LOVELINESS

In "Sir Frances and the Sow," the American poet Galway Kinnell reminds of us the power of self-blessing and of learning to trust our own loveliness.

One of the themes essential to mindfulness practice is the teaching of one's own basic goodness, our essential nature. And yet, one of the first things practitioners notice as we begin to pay attention to the patterns of mind and heart is how critical and judgmental we are of ourselves.

There is often a pervading sense that "I am not enough": "I am not good, kind, patient, smart, beautiful, generous...enough." *Most of the time, we are unconscious of this constant internal monologue of self-doubt and self-judgment, and yet this way of relating to ourselves is one of the greatest harms to our health, vitality and well being.*

Author and mindfulness teacher Tara Brach refers to this as "the trance of unworthiness," which imprisons us in an illusion of separateness and pain, distorting our view of ourselves and of life. *When left unnoticed, this trance of unworthiness can become the automatic lens through which life is viewed, leading to fear, dissatisfaction and a sense of aloneness.* By inclining our mind toward self-care and self-blessing, we can begin to loosen the self-destructive patterns and cultivate compassion, care, kindness and friendliness for ourselves.

We begin to notice how we relate to ourselves, the tone of voice we use to speak to ourselves, the words we say, how we care for ourselves. We begin to see how significantly the way we relate to ourselves colors our perception and we realize that carrying around these negative views and expectations is a burden preventing us from being truly present for ourselves, for others and for life.

────────────┤ MINDFULNESS PRACTICE FOR THE WEEK ├────────────

1. *Each morning when you awaken, set a clear intention to be kind to yourself today.*

2. *Begin to notice the number of times each day you judge or criticize yourself. How does it feel in your body when you notice this? Be careful not to judge yourself for judging. Simply notice, and then make a choice to let the judgment go, returning to your intention of self-kindness.*

3. *Practice saying three kind, acknowledging statements to yourself each day. They can be simple, e.g. "I am grateful that I ate a nutritious lunch today," or, "I was really present for my son this morning." What is most important is not the content of what you say but the process of beginning a new pattern of speaking to yourself with kindness.*

4. *Practice "self-blessing" each night before bed. For example, "May I be peaceful," "May I be safe and protected," "May I be healthy," "May I be happy." You may use any of these phrases or choose phrases that feel most nourishing to you. **Through these practices you are beginning to re-teach yourself your own loveliness.***

21

ROSHI MARSHA LINEHAN, Ph.D. CHOSE THIS QUOTE:

**It is not enough
to be compassionate.
You must act.**

His Holiness the Dalai Lama, 2008

THEME – COMPASSIONATE ACTION

The Oxford dictionary gives several definitions of compassion. "Suffering together with another" and "the feeling or emotion when a person is moved by the suffering or distress of another and by the desire to relieve it" are two such definitions. *Both definitions leave out the actual act of doing something to relieve the suffering of the other.*

When you are the one suffering, compassion alone is simply not enough. Georges Bernanos, a French novelist and political writer, said, "I know the compassion of others is a relief at first. I don't despise it. But it can't quench pain, it slips through your soul as through a sieve." This sums up my thoughts exactly. *Wanting to help another is simply not sufficient. Finding ways to do it, learning what we need to know to relieve others' suffering, developing the skills to be effective — these are what matter at the end of the day.*

When I was a supervisor, I once rebuked a supervisee for reinforcing a client's sense of her own helplessness. The therapist had felt the distress of her client to such a degree that she almost immediately reached out and swept away the event causing the client so much pain. After the rebuke, it was clear my student thought I had no compassion.

So I told her the following story: Imagine a person is standing in hell, standing on coals on fire, jumping up and down and screaming, "Help, help, bring me some water and pour it on my feet! I can't stand this. I am burning up." Then I asked her who she thought was most compassionate — the person who runs to get a pitcher of water and climbs down into hell to pour the water on the poor soul's feet, or the person who rushes down to hell, gets behind the poor soul and pushes, saying "Let's get out of here."

Her answer was remarkable. "Marsha," she said, "the difference between us is that you think you can get people out of hell." Her response was very important because if it were true that she could not help get people out of hell, then she was correct — pouring water would be the wise thing to do.

A year or so later, the therapist called me to thank me. She had learned skills that allowed her to give up on clients less easily in the service of teaching them how to get out of hell.

This story sums up well my passion for evidence-based treatments. It is all too easy to provide a compassionate ear to those in hell. We feel better ourselves and, at times, listening brings temporary relief to the other person. It is undoubtedly better than no relief and occasionally it may really be all that we can offer. But what if we took the time to learn more effective ways to help? What if we all learned the evidence-based treatments that are out there for the learning? What if we insisted that others learn them, not to avoid suffering our clients' pain with them, but to add in actions that are known to help? Would not that be the more compassionate response?

————————{ MINDFULNESS PRACTICE FOR THE WEEK }————————

The mindfulness practices that go with this story are two-fold.

First, *when listening to others in pain, it is important to be mindful of not only the other person's suffering but also of our own.*

Mindfulness of current emotions and sensations is important because through it we learn that indeed we can tolerate both our suffering and that of others. Breathe in and notice sensations of emotion. Breathe out and notice sensations of emotion. Noticing, allowing, in and out.

Second *is the practice of "wise mind". Remind yourself that each of us has the capacity for universal wisdom. It may be difficult to reach, but it is possible. Breathe in deeply, let your mind drop to your center, listen to the silence within, listen in the depth of the emptiness that is itself wisdom. Breathing in and out normally, letting yourself settle into wisdom itself. Asking, at times, questions, listening for an answer (but not answering).*
Breathing in, breathing out, dropping into the silence.

22

CHRIS GERMER, Ph.D. CHOSE THIS QUOTE:

66

Self-care with self-awareness is like learning to breathe underwater.

99

Michael Kearney et al. (2009)

THEME – COMPASSION FATIGUE

When we empathize with the suffering of others, it's real suffering. Our bodies respond as if we were under genuine threat, and with continuous exposure we may show signs of exhaustion, irritation, sleeplessness, or fear. That's compassion fatigue. Compassion fatigue is a sign of being human, not of being weak.

How do we typically care for ourselves when we're exhausted? There are a host of good things we can do, such as taking time off from work, listening to music, and connecting with friends. These strategies generally help to keep our heads above water, but they don't keep us from drowning when we're back at the workplace. That's where compassion and mindfulness training comes in.

"More compassion for compassion fatigue? Are you kidding?" Meditation teacher, Matthieu Ricard, in collaboration with neuroscientist Tanya Singer, suggests that "empathy fatigue" is probably a more accurate expression for "compassion fatigue." Simply feeling the pain of others is a prescription for emotional exhaustion, but "compassion"— empathy plus loving awareness — is actually a positive, energizing emotion. With deep compassion, the sufferings of others occur in a common space of shared humanity and the pain seems to arise and dissipate very much on its own. Perhaps there's no one left to whom the pain can stick.

We all have compassion. Some babies as young as 15 months old show signs of altruism. But we need to dust ourselves off from time to time and return to a natural state. Mindfulness and compassion training is a radical process of letting go of our burdens. We're not trying to be more mindful or compassionate; that's just more work. Instead, we can sit down for a few minutes, see what arises and give ourselves love just because... just because. And then go gently back into the world.

───────┤ MINDFULNESS PRACTICE FOR THE WEEK ├───────

▪

Sit comfortably, close your eyes, and take a few deep breaths.

▪

Scan your body, noting any physical or emotional stress.

▪

Now, aware of the stress you are carrying in your body, inhale fully and deeply, drawing compassion inside your body and filling every cell of your body with compassion. Let yourself be soothed by inhaling deeply.

▪

As you exhale, send out compassion to anyone who is associated with your discomfort, or exhale compassion to the world in general.

▪

Continue breathing compassion in and out, letting your body gradually find a natural, relaxed breathing rhythm.

Section V

{ QUOTES № 23 to 34 }

Important Mindfulness Practices

There are some core mindfulness practices and skills that are found in this section. These teachings help us to be less reactive, more compassionate, and gentler with self and others. These mindfulness practices also help us to be less judgmental, less critical, and more understanding of our own suffering.

23

SHARON SALZBERG CHOSE THIS QUOTE

If you knew as I did the power of giving, you would not let a single meal pass without sharing something.

The Buddha

THEME – THE POWER OF GIVING (GENEROSITY)

Generosity is a matter of spirit. It has little to do with whether or not we have material goods to give or don't. There is always something that we can give to another, for giving is our heart's offering of connection and caring.

In India and Burma I was the recipient of incredible generosity from many people who had very little materially to offer. Yet when they gave, they did so wholeheartedly. People there taught me about generosity, and showed me that it doesn't depend on conventional, external abundance. And if we cannot offer something material, we can give energetically: a smile, our full, undistracted attention.

The Buddha said that no true spiritual life is possible without this kind of generous heart. *Generosity is the very first quality of an awakened mind because of the beautiful quality of joy that arises in an act of true giving. Giving is a happy thing to do: we experience happiness in forming the intention to give, in the actual act of giving and in the recollection of the fact that we have given.* Generosity has been one of my most important personal practices because it reminds me of the capacity of my own heart to go beyond fear ("What if I need that book next week? What if I'm not giving enough?") to honor the power of connection.

┤ MINDFULNESS PRACTICE FOR THE WEEK ├

This is a practice that helps cultivate generosity through awareness: If a strong impulse to give something arises in your mind and it won't cause any harm (like giving away your family's rent money), then make the offering. Stay aware of what is arising in your mind, especially if the next 50 thoughts following the intention to give are fearful, like: "Maybe I'll wear it next year"; "Maybe I will read it after all"; "What if they think I'm stupid for doing this?"
*Let the thoughts go as you remember your motivation, and remember that **generosity is actually a practice, one that implies intentionality, challenges and venturing into new terrain.** Stay aware of your thoughts and feelings after the act of generosity. Are you in fact regretful? Relieved? Buoyant? Let your insights guide your ongoing practice of generosity.*

24

RICK HANSON, Ph.D. CHOSE THIS QUOTE:

66

Anything less than a contemplative perspective on life is an almost certain program for unhappiness.

99

Father Thomas Keating, public lecture, *February 21, 2007, Berkeley, CA*

THEME – THE VALUE OF A CONTEMPLATIVE PERSPECTIVE

By "contemplative," I believe that Father Keating includes prayer, mindfulness with or without reference to God or other transcendental mysteries, and even everyday moments of reflection and gratitude. The common quality at the heart of the contemplative perspective is *awareness* — with receptivity, presence, and an implicit quality of being a friend to yourself.

Why would Father Keating say that unhappiness will most likely come to those who lack some kind of contemplative perspective?

For me, contemplative practices such as meditation help me see clearly — both the world "out there" and my own busy menagerie "in here"— and act more wisely, and feel increasingly grounded in an unconditional happiness and peacefulness in which thoughts and feelings arise and pass away. Without this help, I would surely experience a lot more unhappiness, and cause a lot more trouble for myself and others.

How about you? When you bring a contemplative perspective to a moment or activity, or when you engage contemplative practice more formally, what are the benefits? And when you lose touch with this perspective for a significant period of time, what are the costs?

This reflection can help motivate a person toward a contemplative perspective. You can see and feel its fruits. You can also know – substantiated by many studies – that your own contemplative perspective and practices will gradually change your brain for the better, building neural tissues and increasing activity in regions that control attention, tune into your own feelings and those of others, and cool down negative emotions. And you can appreciate how the benefits of a contemplative perspective ripples through you and beyond you to touch others in ways seen and unseen.

{ MINDFULNESS PRACTICE FOR THE WEEK }

So, this week, I suggest that you commit to one or more minutes a day of some kind of contemplative practice. You could follow your breath. Or be aware of beauty around you. Or stand outside under the stars. Or walk or do yoga or exercise with sustained mindfulness to the movements of your body. Or connect to your sense of something transcendental, whatever you may call it — such as God, Spirit, Buddhanature, the Mystery, or by no name at all – and open to its presence.

You can practice by yourself or with others. But keep your promise to yourself of one minute or more a day. I have this promise to myself and almost always keep it, even if it's the last few minutes before my head hits the pillow.

Whatever you do, both do it and be aware of the experience of it, and its fruits. Take in the benefits, even subtle or mild ones: as you sink into your practice, feel that its gifts are sinking into you. Let these benefits draw you toward contemplation, inclining your mind increasingly in its direction.

As a contemplative perspective takes root in your heart, let it grow and branch out into ordinary activities. What's it like to do dishes, drive a car, or write emails within a broader framework of sustained awareness, untroubled by the contents – sensations, sounds, thoughts, desires, etc. – flowing through it? If there are benefits here as well, let these sink into you, too.

Most fundamentally, make sanctuary for the contemplative qualities that are meaningful to you. Even if you drift from them for days or even years, as I have, you can always come back, and find your way home.

25

RICHARD FIELDS, Ph.D. CHOSE THIS QUOTE:

❝

The thought manifests as the word;
The word manifests as the deed;
The deed develops into habit;
And habit hardens into character.

So watch the thought and
its ways with care
And let it spring from love,
Born out of concern for all beings.

❞

The Buddha

THEME – BEING LESS CRITICAL OF OTHERS

The Buddha reminds us that the cycle of criticism starts with the critical thought. You can look at being critical of others as a thought disorder, and something that requires a more mindful attitude.

This quote also reminds us that criticizing, gossiping about and judging others can become a very hurtful habit. Being critical is a reactive defense to protect ourselves from being hurt, or having trust violated (betrayal). Ironically, we are doing exactly what we don't want others to do to us by being critical.

Being critical of others distracts us from being present and having an open heart.

When you are critical of others, that could be a signal that you are upset with yourself. So it is better to just work on yourself.

A parody of the Alcoholics Anonymous serenity prayer says this well.

> *"Grant me the serenity to accept the people I cannot change,*
> *Courage to change the one I can,*
> *And the wisdom to know it's me."*
>
> Anonymous

{ MINDFULNESS PRACTICE FOR THE WEEK }

If you find you are being critical, slow down, stop and
refocus on being more concerned, caring and compassionate.

The third path of the Buddhist eight-fold path is "right speech".

It is said that words can help create peace or wars, invoke compassion or hatred, affirmation or shame, join or divide, love or destroy. Right speech involves words of honesty, kindness and nurturance. Right speech involves speaking only what is worthy and valuable.

Guidelines for right speech involve telling the truth, speaking gently with warmth and friendliness. Mindful or right speech is described as "aesthetically" pleasing like a work of art.

This week practice right speech to counter criticism. Metaphorically see yourself playing a harp in harmony with others, rather than wildly and erratically slamming the drums of criticism.

RICHARD FIELDS, Ph.D. CHOSE THIS QUOTE:

66

If you get angry easily, it may be
because the seed of anger in you
has been watered frequently
over many years, and unfortunately
you have allowed it or even
encouraged it be watered.

99

Thich Nhat Hanh, Taming the Tiger Within, *2004*

THEME – DEALING WITH ANGER

This quote is important because anger blocks connection and goodness.

Unfortunately anger has been planted or seeded from generation to generation. The habit of responding with anger is reinforced (watered) with each angry incident.

Anger is a difficult emotion to tame because it has some very powerful addictive physiological and psychological reinforcers. You can even find yourself trying to justify your anger because it is hard to control.

I have counseled many people who have suffered significantly, and lost a lot because of their anger and anger related behavior. *The sooner they work on their anger and resentments, and stop blaming others, progress begins.*

The word HALTS stands for being hungry, angry, lonely, tired, sick. It is used to remind the person in alcohol/drug recovery that when they are in HALTS, they are more vulnerable to relapse. You are also more prone to respond in strong anger, when you are in HALTS.

The goal is to not water anger. By not succumbing to anger you slowly weaken it. As time goes on, it becomes easier to reduce your "habit of anger". Rather than having a heavy heart when angry, you can instead have an open heart and practice goodness of heart, self-compassion and compassion for others.

If you do get angry, don't beat yourself up about it. It is a lapse, which is normal, and it means there is more work to be done.

{ MINDFULNESS PRACTICE FOR THE WEEK }

REDUCING ANGER

This week focus on reducing your anger. Recognize when you are in HALTS and act accordingly by trying to wait until you are out of HALTS to deal with issues. Recognize what sparks your anger. Notice how frequently you have little flare-ups of emotion or anger. See how well you do at recognizing your "hot buttons" (e.g. money issues, politics, relationship issues, bad drivers, etc.) Resist feeding these anger flare-ups, so the fire of anger is not sparked.

27

TARA BRACH, Ph.D. CHOSE THIS QUOTE:

"

Our failure to know joy is a direct reflection of our inability to forgive.

"

Charlotte Joko Beck

THEME – PRACTICING FORGIVENESS

Forgiveness is a wonderful idea — until we really have something to forgive. When we have been betrayed and wounded, when we are threatened and afraid, holding onto resentment is a way of protecting ourselves. It is our way of armoring against the experience of raw pain.

Consider where you might be carrying resentment or blame. What would happen if you stopped believing your story of someone being wrong or bad? What's the most difficult thing you'd have to experience? *For most of us, when we put down our story of wrongdoing, we are forced to feel our powerlessness and vulnerability, our hurt and fear.* There's a good reason we hold so tightly to our hatred and anger. Yet we have an inner wisdom that intuits the suffering inherent in an unforgiving heart. In a movie called *The Interpreter* (2005), this wisdom is expressed in a short phrase:

"Vengeance is a lazy form of grief."

Vengeance is also a lazy form of fear and hurt. *It is "lazy" in the sense that it's easier to lash out than to feel our suffering.* Yet ultimately this aggression does not serve us. We have to bring presence to our wounded heart if we are to heal and live fully. In the words of Zen teacher Charlotte Joko Beck, "We forgive for the freedom of our own hearts." Forgiving doesn't mean that we become passive in the face of harmful behavior. It may be that we forgive but dedicate ourselves to never letting that harm happen again. We may forgive but maintain very strong boundaries to protect ourselves or others. *Forgiving simply means that we are unwilling to put another person — or ourselves — out of our heart.*

Forgiving is a lifetime practice. We regularly close and tighten against others, and we are often at war with ourselves. Yet we can learn to recognize when we've constricted and then to connect with our intention to forgive. Our sincere intention alone begins to open the door. The full process of forgiving may require the support of healers, therapists and friends, or we might do it alone. Either way, gradually we'll find that we are letting go with increasing ease. *We are more at home in an undefended heart, a heart that is free to love without holding back.*

{ MINDFULNESS PRACTICE FOR THE WEEK }

Scan your life and identify and list those people toward whom you are carrying resentment. For a week, or as long as it takes, select one of these people and let your intention be to loosen the mental habit of blame.

When you become aware of blaming thoughts, pause.
Without any self-judgment, become curious about what lies under blame.
Ask yourself: If I had to let go of this resentment, what unpleasant feelings would be there? Feel your body and sense what is true. Is there fear, self-blame, powerlessness? In these moments, simply bring a compassionate presence to whatever is arising in you.

What is your experience of yourself when you shift from blaming another person to a kind presence with your own experience? What is the quality of your heart? Your awareness?

Remind yourself that releasing blame and resentment is the pathway to an unconditionally loving heart.

28

PHILLIP MOFFITT CHOSE THIS QUOTE:

"

Even after all this time, The Sun never says to the Earth, 'You owe me.' Look what happens With a love like that, It lights the whole sky.

"

Hafiz, 14th-century Persian poet

THEME – The Tyranny of Expectations

In daily life, your mind is filled with expectations that largely determine which events you pay attention to and how you interpret them. *Most of the time, you are unconscious of your expectations, yet they control much of what you do and pose an obstacle to living from your intentions.* Unfortunately, when they're left unnoticed, expectations can become all-powerful and cause you to have negative views about yourself and others that can manifest as confusion, disappointment, fear, defeat, dissatisfaction or defensiveness. *They may plague your daily life, causing you to be irritable, disillusioned and anxious. And they can lead you to speak or act unskillfully and to make poor decisions. I call this effect "the tyranny of expectations," since they can literally kill your joy and distort your view of life.*

As you become mindful of expectations, you start to see how they dominate your life choices and color your perception. You begin to see that many of them are just views and opinions that you created or others created for you. You see that, to a large degree, life happens independent of and often contrary to your expectations. At first this may seem dismaying, but as you develop more and more awareness, *you eventually start to realize that carrying around this jumble of expectations in your head is a burden and that it gets in the way of being present for and responding to the life you have.*

A critical step in gaining clarity around expectations is learning to distinguish between expectations and possibilities. Expectations assume a certain result and are future-based. They hold your present sense of well-being hostage to a future that may or may not happen. When you are controlled by your expectations, you are living a contingent life and, therefore, aren't free in the present moment. In contrast to expectations, *possibilities are based in the present moment where you're alive to the mystery of life. Being open to exploring possibilities stimulates the mind, makes life interesting and provides you with the energy and motivation to live as fully as you can in the present moment based on your intentions.*

┤ Mindfulness Practice for the Week ├

1. *Over the next few days, track how many times an expectation arises, including any hidden assumptions. Each time you spot an expectation, ask yourself, "Is this helpful or not?"*

2. *Begin to notice the number of times each day that you feel the pressure of someone else's expectations of you. How does it feel when you encounter these expectations? What does your mind do with them?*

3. *Decide whether you want to make releasing expectations an active part of your mindfulness practice. If the answer is yes, then start to release some of the small expectations that you carry. And then gradually start to work on those larger expectations to which you are really attached.*

Adapted from *Emotional Chaos to Clarity: How to Live More Skillfully, Make Better Decisions, and Find Purpose in Life,* by Phillip Moffitt (Penguin, 2012).

29

RICHARD FIELDS, Ph.D. CHOSE THIS QUOTE:

"

Time is a flying bird. Do you want to
capture the bird and encage it?
Then you need patience.
Your fondest dreams will be
transformed into fruitful realities
if you just know the secret of
growing the patience-tree in your heart.

"

Sri Chinmoy, The Wisdom of Sri Chinmoy, *2000*

THEME – PATIENCE

How many relationships, experiences and opportunities were washed away by the flash flood of impatience?

In this world of instant information and communication, immediate satisfaction, quick change and desire for constant satisfaction, one can be driven to impulsivity that may satisfy the short term while sacrificing long-term benefits.

We often need to give things time to develop, change and/or heal. *Timing is an important factor in transformation.*

─{ MINDFULNESS PRACTICE FOR THE WEEK }─

*The Alcoholics Anonymous proverb "Progress not perfection",
helps us to remember to be patient, rest in uncertainty,
and not to be attached to outcome.*

*Issues of control, anxiety, and expectations of others can get
in the way of patience. We certainly can be excited and have energy
about things, but directing that energy in a more purposeful
and patient way can lead to more benefits.*

*Pausing and having patience creates more sensitivity and
compassion for others. We sometimes need to give our children,
our partners, out colleagues time to come to their own
conclusions without forcing them to see our way.*

*Counting to 10, when frustrated, often helps, and being
quiet when sensing you are getting nowhere.
Another Alcoholics Anonymous proverb reminds us that
it is often not worth the conflict to prove you are right —
"Would you rather be right, or happy?"*

This week practice more patience and less reactivity.

30

LARRY CAMMARATA, Ph.D. CHOSE THIS QUOTE:

The soft overcomes the hard;
the gentle overcomes the rigid.
Everyone knows this is true,
but few can put it into practice.

Lao Tzu, Tao Te Ching, *6th century BC*

THEME – HARMONIZING – QIGONG & TAI CHI

This ancient quote, attributed to the Chinese sage Lao Tzu, contains pragmatic teachings about health, relationships and mindfulness of the body that are integral to the practices of Tai Chi and Qigong. In the martial art of Tai Chi, the practitioner uses softness to receive, absorb and redirect the aggression of an adversary. *In the meditative movement practice of Qigong, the practitioner learns to soften the belly, relax deeply and breathe calmly, while standing firmly.*

Harmony is a central principle of practices such as Qigong and Tai Chi. I prefer the term "harmonizing", as it implies a relational process that is always changing. Through the dynamic process of harmonizing, one can transform distress and conflict in relationships into acceptance, honoring, and softness.

In mindfulness practice, softness implies nonjudgmental observation and loving acceptance of painful experiences that are sometimes encountered.

When we soften or intentionally relax into our painful thoughts and feelings, reactive rigidity and tension can be transformed into gentleness.

─────────────{ MINDFULNESS PRACTICE FOR THE WEEK }─────────────

Consistent practice can transform the words upon this page into an embodied skill. Here are some questions and recommendations for exploration:

In this moment, where are you holding tension in your body? If possible, soften and relax that part of your body. If not possible, imagine the softening occurring.

What or who have you been recently resisting or negatively judging? Experiment with dropping the resistance or judgment in the moment it occurs; relax into the experience and notice what arises.

How can softness and gentleness inform, support and empower your work, self-care, exercise and relationships?

Practice standing firmly with feet connected to the ground while dropping and relaxing your shoulders, softening your belly, breathing calmly and smiling.

31

AMY WEINTRAUB, MFA, ERYT-500 CHOSE THIS QUOTE:

66

Yoga attempts to create a state in which we are always present – really present – in every action, in every moment."

99

T.K.V. Desikachar, The Heart of Yoga: Developing a Personal Practice, *1995*

THEME – SELF AWARENESS – YOGA

I like to remind my students as they practice yoga that the body is always present, while the mind is a time traveler. So when you bring your attention to the sensations in your body as you practice postures, you become the presence you seek. That moment of presence is a window through to whatever mood is visiting or whatever story you happen to be telling yourself. *As the practice becomes established, the window widens into a door you can walk through, simply by pausing to notice sensation.*

Certainly, you can practice yoga in a numbed out sort of way, moving through the motions, not feeling. But what I'm talking about is a mindful practice of yoga that brings the attention to breath and sensation. *When you practice Yoga with awareness of the sensations in your body, your thoughts and your feelings, you will grow in self-awareness.*

And as you grow in self-awareness, you begin to have glimpses of what it means to feel utterly and wholly connected. The moments of awareness may be like slender threads that you follow as you release from a Yoga posture.

But as your practice deepens, the threads begin to weave together, and you may begin to carry this awareness with you off the mat — maybe for just a few minutes after your session, then through much of the day.

Eventually, you may keep this awareness with you always. You may remain aware of your wholeness, who you are beneath the social mask or the professional mask. The cultivation of self-awareness through your practice is *the ultimate goal of Yoga practice—to become a* jivan mukti, *an awakened one. You will remember that beneath the temporary separation you may be feeling, you are whole.*

┤ MINDFULNESS PRACTICE FOR THE WEEK ├

MOUNTAIN POSE (TADASANA)

Stand with your feet parallel and a few inches apart. Find your deep yogic breath, breathing through the nostrils to the bottom lungs so that you feel your belly expanding. Make a light, soothing ocean sound, like a baby's snore. See if you can cultivate an even breath, four counts on the inhalation and four counts to exhale.

Ground into the four corners of your feet. Engage the muscles of the legs, thighs and those around the knees, without locking the knees. Scoop the tailbone towards the ground, leveling the pelvis. Lift your torso out of your waist and draw your shoulders down and back.

Slowly begin to lift your arms out to your sides and then bring your arms over your head with the palms facing each other. Relax your shoulders down again. If there is discomfort in the shoulders, bend your elbows. Continue breathing long and deep through the nostrils, filling with life breath — prana. Feel as though you are holding your arms up, not from your shoulders, but from the core of your body.

Ground your feet and experience your connection to the earth. Feel the energy pulsing between your hands. Notice sensation in your shoulders, your arms. Sense deeply into your face — sense the radiance in your lips, your cheeks, your eyes. Focus on your breath. Relax into the sensation that's strong in your body. Bring the breath there. Bring the attention there and dive through that window of sensation into a deeper experience of being in your physical body in this moment, in Yoga, in union. Allow your breath to fill this vessel you've been given, strengthening it so that you can hold more energy, more joy, expanding your chest, your heart, your lungs, so that there's more room inside for you.

When you feel complete, slowly release the pose, lowering your arms to your sides. Stand with your feet a comfortable distance apart, your eyes closed and your arms at your sides, palms face out. Sense deeply into the sensations in your arms, your hands, your palms. Feel the radiance in your palms. **The body is always present. When you can bring your attention to the sensation in your body, you become the presence you seek.**

32

Rubin Naiman, Ph.D. chose this quote:

Nothing is so intolerable to man as being fully at rest.

Blaise Pascal, Pensées, *1662*

THEME – VALUING REST

"I don't think so," is a common refrain I hear when sharing this quote with others. "I love to rest." And they quickly add, "I enjoy reading, watching TV, hiking or catching a good movie." Others assert they just love to kick back with a glass of wine, a martini or a joint. *So many of us confuse rest with recreation and even with inebriation.*

Confusing a call to rest with a need for a quick fix of energy, many others reflexively respond to feeling tired by refueling. We seek fuel in the form of highly processed carbohydrates, stimulating beverages and even gratuitous drama. *So many of us confuse our need for rest with a need for stimulation.*

It's not a surprise that, deprived of rest, we literally become *rest-less*. We are uneasy, nervous and agitated. Too often we mistake restlessness for passion and then complain of boredom when we start to slow down.

If it's not about recreation, inebriation, overstimulation or restlessness, then what is rest? As a sleep specialist, this is a question I've pondered for years. I see rest as a natural state of open and relaxed receptivity, a tranquil or yin-imbued state of consciousness. Technically, rest is characterized by alpha brain wave activity and is also the bridge between waking and sleep. *Just as we must learn to walk before we can run, we must learn to rest before we can sleep well, or wake well.* The tranquility we obtain from true rest can also gently modulate our waking activity.

Why are we so resistant to rest? Well, when we finally do hit the brakes and slow down, everything we've stashed in the back of the wagon comes flying forward. All of the unfinished psychological business of our lives, small and large, will arise opportunistically when we slow and stop. If we truly want to rest, we must be ready to negotiate this.

{ MINDFULNESS PRACTICE FOR THE WEEK }

From meditation to prayer and high-tech methods to guided imagery, there are a great many ways to formally practice resting. In addition to such a formal rest practice, I encourage you to intentionally infuse your daily life with restfulness. Tap gently on the brakes. Slow down a little. **Walk and drive and even talk a bit more slowly than usual.** *Install an imaginary personal speedometer to be mindful of your pace throughout the day.* **When you find yourself speedy or restless, rest.** *Take a moment to slow, sit, stop, pause, breathe. Become mindful of the restfulness that always patiently awaits you in the background. Rest is not the opposite of activity; it is its foundation.*

33

FRANK OSTASESKI CHOSE THIS QUOTE:

"

I slept and dreamt that life was joy, I woke and found that life was service, I acted and behold service was joy."

"

Rabindranath Tagore

THEME – GIVING SERVICE

Life calls us to service — caring for an aging parent, being a community volunteer, working for social justice, dedicating our efforts to a good cause. *Service is our innate love, wisdom and generosity carried into action. Taken as a practice of awareness, service becomes a natural expression of our interdependence.*

While service is natural, even instinctual, it isn't always easy. The most difficult and persistent roadblock is the illusion of our sense of separate self. Too often we're busy playing out a habitual role or trying to confirm a familiar sense of self instead of recognizing what might really serve. If we're not careful, this tendency will imprison us and those we serve.

Mindfulness practice is in part the cultivation of an openness in which this self-centeredness dissolves. The more open we are, the more willing we are to love and serve. This comes from the recognition that we are actually one being. It's no longer a question of giving. *True service is always mutually beneficial. In caring for others we nurture ourselves.* If the right hand gets hurt, the left hand compassionately reaches out in support. It's nothing special really, just simple human kindness. *In this light, service is a joyful exertion of who we are.*

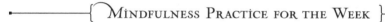

MINDFULNESS PRACTICE FOR THE WEEK

There are opportunities to serve everywhere. We need only be open and respond to what life is presenting. What is calling? How will you answer? **When the heart is undivided, everything we encounter becomes our practice. Service becomes a sacred exchange like breathing in and breathing out.**

How will you serve? Listen to a friend's grief with an open heart? Water a thirsty plant? Reassure a frightened child? Sign a political petition? Feed the hungry? Be a calm presence in the midst of chaos? These are all acts of service.

Try to observe yourself in the moment of thought, feeling and action. Afterwards, look within and ask yourself a few questions.

■

What was my first response to the call of service?

■

How did my sense of separate self limit my capacity to serve?

■

How did openness guide my actions?

■

What did I notice about the shared experience of service?

34

SUSAN KAISER-GREENLAND, JD CHOSE THIS QUOTE:

"

'Lots of people talk to animals,' said Pooh. 'Maybe, but...' 'Not very many listen, though,' he said. 'That's the problem,' he added.

"

A.A. Milne, Winnie the Pooh, *1926*

THEME – SKILL IN LISTENING

Children's books are a surprising source of wisdom, and there are no wiser characters in literature than those who inhabit the Hundred Acre Wood in A. A. Milne's *Winnie the Pooh*. *There is no doubt that Pooh and his friends have brought mindfulness into their daily lives.* Consider, for example, this delightful exchange between Piglet and Pooh: "It's today!' squealed Piglet. 'My favorite day,' said Pooh." And then there's Pooh's proclamation, *"Rivers know this: there is no hurry. We shall get there some day."*

It was hard to choose one piece of Pooh wisdom, but I ultimately selected this passage on listening because it is one of the most powerful practices we can engage in. Listening translates directly to everyday life by giving us an opportunity to practice being fully present with family, friends and colleagues. By listening, on purpose, *we build awareness of what's happening in our outside worlds* while, at the same time, building awareness of what's happening in our inner worlds.

───────{ MINDFULNESS PRACTICE FOR THE WEEK }───────

The listening practice that I offer for this week is a simple one: Listening, on purpose, to the sound of the rain. It's simple but not always that easy. If it's not raining outside, you can practice anyway by listening to the sound of a waterfall or even a cd or mp3 file. In the instructions below I mention listening to rain, but the sound of any moving water is fine.

Have you ever seen waves rise and fall in the ocean, and heard the sound of their crash when they roll onto the beach? Meditation teachers often suggest we view the activity of our minds much as we would view waves in the ocean: that we watch them rise, then watch them crest, and watch them fall and ultimately fade away.

There is one thing that is absolutely predictable about both rain and waves — both of them will change. In this practice we listen to the sound of the rain on purpose and with curiosity. When we place our full attention on the sound of the rain, something remarkable tends to happen. **First we notice that it changes, how it changes and when it changes.** *Next, we often notice that the thoughts, emotions and feelings in our bodies change too. Our thoughts and emotions tend to quiet and our bodies tend to relax. Let's practice together and find out.*

Find a comfortable posture seated or lying down. If you like it, put your hands on your belly. Notice how your body feels right now. Feel the breath moving in and out of your body, then shift your

attention for a moment to your whole body. With your attention,
scan the top of your head to the tips of your toes. Notice if
you find tension or discomfort anywhere and if you do,
you might want to find a more comfortable position before we begin.

Let's rest for a while and listen to the rain on purpose.
You might notice that your mind wanders; that's what minds
do after all. If that happens, simply notice you're distracted
and shift your attention back to the sound of the rain.

If it's tough to keep your mind on the sounds, you can shift
your attention back to feeling the movement of breath in your body.
The idea is to bring your mind back to a single sensation
and hold it there until your attention stabilizes. Once your
attention is stable, you can open your attention and
listen to the sound of the rain again.

Resting in this moment you might want to see if anything is changing.

The sound is changing but how? Is the thunder coming
in and out? Is it raining harder and louder?

Is anything changing in your body? Does your breathing
feel the same as it did when you started?

Is your attention changing? Is the quality of your
attention the same — alert, dull, easy —
or is the quality of your attention changing too?

When you're ready to close your practice, I encourage
you to do so gently and gradually. Many people
close bringing to mind an image of one person or
group of people and wishing them well.

Listening to the sound of the rain or other water sounds
is one of my all-time favorite practices and I hope you
enjoy it too. When we get right down to it, our practice
can be this simple, this peaceful and this easy to integrate
into what's already happening in our everyday lives.

Section VI

{ QUOTES № 35 TO 39 }

Being in Difficult Life Situations: Stress & Suffering

Life involves suffering. Mindfulness helps us to better deal with difficult life and death situations, stress, and suffering.

SYLVIA BOORSTEIN, Ph.D., LCSW CHOSE THIS QUOTE:

"

I am the cause of most of my suffering because of the habits of my own mind.

"

His Holiness the Dalai Lama

THEME – SELF-INDUCED SUFFERING

My favorite scene in *Kundun*, the 1997 Hollywood film about the life of the current Dalai Lama, is the one in which he, as a child of perhaps eight years, is being quizzed by his tutors on The Four Noble Truths. His recitation of the first Truth, that of the ubiquitous nature of suffering, is deemed adequate. The child then says, as his recitation of the second Truth, "The cause of suffering is craving." His tutors stop him. They say, "Too much ego." The young Dalai Lama seems to reflect briefly and then says, "I am the cause of most of my suffering because of the habits of my own mind."

That is a remarkable insight for an eight year old. It is a remarkable insight for a 40 year old. It is a liberating insight for anyone at any age. I suffer because of the habits of my mind that allow the sense that things should be different from how they are to take over my mind.

Of course, I often wish that things were different. I wish I had more or less of this or that. I wish I'd gotten the job I wanted, or that my children had made happy career choices, or that there was world peace. We all wish. It is in the nature of discriminating minds to wish.

What creates the sense of suffering for me, and I think for everyone, is the feeling that my mind cannot relax and accommodate the truth of my experience *unless* it is what I wanted. Perhaps the most painful habit I have is that of delusion, of imagining that somehow I am in charge of how things turn out. I'm not. *My wishes, and my actions, have something to do with what happens to me. Ultimately, however, I am not in charge.* I keep learning this lesson over and over again, both by paying attention in meditation and by paying attention to my life, but when my mind is startled or overwhelmed by stress, I forget.

I also have the habit of excessive fretting and worrying, imagining the worst. The habit of delusion is pretty much universal, but the habit of fretting is particular — not everyone has it. I think it is partly genetic, partly the result of traumatic life circumstances. It is a habit that skews perception in such a way that neutral circumstances appear as potential threats. My meditation practice has illuminated this habit for me to the extent that I am usually able to recognize it as a factor in a moment of sensed jeopardy and correct for it, just as a color blind person knows how to recognize a red light by the section of the traffic signal that is brighter. The fact that I have a disproportionate number of fretful thoughts compared to other people hasn't vanished, even with a lot of meditation practice. I still consider my mindfulness practice a success because the habit is less disturbing.

Other people have the habit of easily becoming angered, or easily losing confidence, or easily being overtaken by sensual desire, or easily becoming overwhelmed. I don't think we get to choose our main habit. I think our habits are part of the package we are born with, like eye color or body type. Indeed, now that I recognize my fretfulness as a habit, one of what the Buddha names as the five principle hindrances to clear understanding, I am content with it.

I even like it better than other disruptive habits. Perhaps, though, that's because I am used to it and therefore sure it is manageable.

In *Kundun*, which I watch every year or so because it is so well done, the young child Dalai Lama goes on to add the third and fourth of the truths of suffering, that of the promise of the end of suffering being a possibility and the naming of the Eightfold Path of practice as the means to cultivating peace of mind. I'm sure they are wonderfully rendered as well, but the line that stays with me and that I use most to teach with is the one I chose to highlight here: "I am the cause of most of my suffering because of the habits of my own mind."

{ MINDFULNESS PRACTICE FOR THE WEEK }

"May I meet this moment fully. May I meet it as a friend."
"This is what is happening, and it is painful."

I like to recite these two phrases to myself as I begin a practice of sitting meditation and/or at any time that I become aware of the fact that my mind has filled with suffering:

"May I meet this moment fully. May I meet it as a friend."

This reminds me that suffering is the unrecognized or unacknowledged tension of imperative. The antidote to the suffering is recognizing it and meeting it with wisdom and compassion:

"This is what is happening, and it is painful."

36

ELISHA GOLDSTEIN, Ph.D. CHOSE THIS QUOTE:

66

Don't turn away. Keep your gaze on the bandaged place. That's where the light enters you.

99

Rumi, 13th-century Sufi poet

THEME – BEING WITH SUFFERING

In one of my favorite quotes, Rumi points to a universal truth of healing: The way to emotional freedom is through being with and embracing that which is painful or difficult in us rather than trying to fix, push away or run from it.

Now, there's nothing wrong with trying to fix things. Without this ability, you wouldn't have the seat you're sitting in, the computer you're looking at or the clothes you're wearing (if you're wearing them). Most of the time we're not even aware we're trying to avoid things.

However, when it comes to our emotions, trying to think our way out of them is only a path of avoidance. This avoidance creates further suffering.

Think about it for a second. What happens when you try and think about becoming less anxious or depressed? You go up into your head and start swirling around about why this is happening and maybe what you can do about it. In other words, we add stress to discomfort.

It is in the very moment that we become intimate, in a nonjudgmental way, with our discomfort that we send the message internally that we care about ourselves ("the light enters you"). This begins to transform the moment.

{ Mindfulness Practice for the Week }

***When you experience an uncomfortable feeling,
try this experiment for a single minute:***

"Breathing in, I feel this feeling; breathing out, I let it be"

*You can shorten this to just saying
"feel" on the in breath and "let be" on the out breath.*

*The instructions are simple, but the practice may not always be easy.
Be kind and gentle with yourself through this process.*

37

POLLY YOUNG-EISENDRATH, Ph.D. CHOSE THIS QUOTE:

"

Life is suffering.

"

The Buddha, First Noble Truth

THEME – DEALING WITH DIFFICULT SITUATIONS – DUKKHA

When they hear the first teaching of the Buddha, known as The First Noble Truth, many people feel it expresses a pessimistic view. "Suffering" is the English word that is typically used to translate the Sanskrit term *Dukkha*. *Dukkha refers to a quality of experience that cannot be translated directly into English. It refers to a quality of off-centeredness or being out of balance like a wheel riding off its axle or a bone out of its socket. A contemporary translation of "stress" or "stressfulness" best captures the meaning, but it also makes sense to offer a string of words — such as pain, misery, anguish, stress, suffering — to suggest the range of meanings associated with Dukkha.*

In his supreme enlightenment, the Buddha saw that Dukkha is built into our lives; Dukkha is rooted in our condition of impermanence and the complex contingencies of our interdependence in this world.

Teachings on, and practices of, mindfulness – paying close attention to moment-to-moment experience with a gentle matter-of-fact awareness – help us develop the skills we need to deal with and transform Dukkha. As we come to do this more effectively in our everyday lives, we see the First Noble Truth in a new light that transforms our view of pain, misery, anguish, stress, suffering.

Since 2004, I have had an unwelcome opportunity in my personal life to test the strength of my Buddhist practice that had matured for more than three decades. My husband and best friend of 26 years has lost his mind to early-onset Alzheimer's disease. At 63, he now lives in a serene and comfortable residential care center about an hour away. I live alone — with a big dog — in the Vermont countryside. Ed functions at the cognitive level of about four years old and his impairment increases as the months pass. He and I are divorced for financial and psychological reasons. I go out to see him twice a week, a drive that takes me through the mountains at night. And yes, he recognizes me and reaches out with warmth and need. We are affectionate though not intimate. *He's a lovely soul, but I can no longer see myself in his eyes because he cannot hold me in his mind.* And yet, I am happy for his happiness. Ironically, Ed is clearly happier now than he has ever been. He feels secure, his needs are taken care of, nothing is demanded of him and he is busy with the daily activities of the center.

As for me, I wouldn't say that I am lonely; my life is full. I have lots of fascinating things to do (largely because I still need to earn a living and my work is interesting) and four wonderfully feisty, grown children (two biological and two step-children) and four grandchildren. I travel and have a busy work schedule. I am vital and healthy and full of ideas about what life and love mean. I would like to fall in love again and I have come to know how precious it is to really know and deeply accept another particular human being who is an equal and an intimate.

During the time of my greatest sorrow, in the years of financial ruin and confusion that were synchronous with getting Ed's diagnosis clarified, I was comforted by three things: my Buddhist practice, my dearest friends and the songs of Zen teacher and singer-song-writer Leonard Cohen. He was my love-guru. His music and his spiritual teachings through song were the only musical food I could consume.

In his song *Villanelle for Our Time* (2004), Cohen sings,

> "From bitter searching of the heart
> Quickened with passion and with pain
> We rise to play a greater part."

Here is a masterful teaching on the Buddha's First Noble Truth: we engage the "bitter searching of the heart" in order to "rise to play a greater part." *Our sufferings, losses, stresses, flaws, mistakes, failures, pain and anguish are all DOORS that open.* When we walk through them without refusing, without narrating them falsely as victimizing us, then ironically we are happier than we thought we could be... than we imagined was possible.

{ MINDFULNESS PRACTICE FOR THE WEEK }

The meditation practices I find most useful in times of crisis are twofold: first, mindfulness of change and resting states in body sensations; and second, contemplation of the meaning of Dukkha. Mindfulness of body sensations provides a base for noting the arising and passing of immediate conditions. I do formal practices for an hour several days per week or for at least 10 minutes (to remind my awareness) on days when I have limited time. I bring these skills with me when I read, chant and listen (for example, to Leonard Cohen) to teachings about how unwelcome change can open our hearts to compassion.

Alzheimer's? People dread it. And of course, I am not recommending it; the disease has brought tragedy into the life of Ed, my family and me. Once it was accepted as a part of our lives, though, the situation was not a "disaster." It quickened our hearts with passion and pain as we went on engaging with life — including, most prominently, Ed. As a result of his decades of meditation and Buddhist practice, Ed embraced his situation. At one point, a couple of years ago, he even said, "This disease has made me spiritual." Now he's a daily example to the 20 other residents at his care center. He's an example to the staff. He's happy and open and full of good spirits and hugs and kisses. He often says, "I am a lucky man!"

From my side, I am beginning to reach out for love in my personal life again. I have been "dating"— getting to know strangers. I am finding out a great deal about what I value in a love-candidate: how generosity and kindness and humor, even a charming wit, are at the core of my attraction. I can take my love for Ed forward. I still love Ed and I can expand that love to include others.

Increasingly, I recite a passage from another Cohen song,
"The Heart with no Companion" (2008):

"I greet you from the other side
Of sorrow and despair
With a love so vast and shattered
It will reach you everywhere"

These words memorialize a shift in view from the belief that loss is
"a disaster" to the perspective that change, even when deeply unwelcome,
is just change. We can come to know that nothing can defeat our love.
As we are faced with misery, adversity, ignominy and other sufferings, our
mindful acceptance of them breaks our hearts into countless compassionate
sparks that reach out to everything with warmth and light.

In reality, there is nothing to fear as long as we can fully embrace,
again and again, the emergence of life and vitality. And now I know,
more deeply than I could have ever imagined, that when we reach
out for love, when we vow to love another — beast, partner, child,
woman or man — we promise to break our heart. In love, we always
lose because our beloved will disappear, leave, be erased or separated
from us. And for this reason, love is blessed and our beloved is precious.

38

WILLIAM MORGAN, PSY.D. CHOSE THIS QUOTE:

66

There is a very simple secret to being happy. Just cease your demand on this moment.

99

The Buddha, Adyashanti

THEME – SELF-CREATED UNHAPPINESS

Moment-to-moment mindfulness is easy to describe but difficult to practice. There is a narcissistic injury involved here, as we have mastered more complex tasks in our lives and find it embarrassing to be "failing" at something so seemingly straightforward.

As a result, a common tendency is to use excessive effort to hold the attention steady on the subject of meditation. While this approach may be effective for a couple of minutes, it soon creates tension. As this becomes unpleasant, the mind begins to look for greener pastures, generally through reflecting or daydreaming. When this is noticed, self-judgment may arise, and further efforts are made to return to the object of meditation, which in turn creates further tension.

I believe that the inability to step back and see this self-defeating pattern — and the demand it is placing on the present moment — is a primary reason for the struggle to establish a regular mediation practice. Why would I want to create additional tension and a sense of failure on a daily basis?

This cycle is a near-at-hand microcosm of *dukkha, the truth of self-related unhappiness,* which can be summarized as wanting something other than what is present to be there, or attempting to freeze frame the present moment of experience.

According to the Buddha, this is the very pattern which needs to be investigated and changed in order to find deeper contentment and freedom! When this is clearly understood, the following practice approach becomes possible.

────────{ MINDFULNESS PRACTICE FOR THE WEEK }────────

■

Establish a relaxing flow of breath. Notice how difficult it is to give oneself permission to do this.

■

While maintaining this state of relaxation, allow the attention to move freely in a flow of open awareness.

■

Notice when a "demand on the moment", in the name of meditation, begin to create tension. This will usually involve an intention to move away from some aspect of present experience, or an effort to fixate the mind in a particular state.

■

When this is noticed, reestablish a relaxing flow of breath (step 1) before opening the awareness once again (step 2).

It is critical to see how we bring our striving and perfectionist tendencies into mediations, or they will fly under the radar and further create the very suffering we wish to alleviate.

39

FRANK OSTASESKI CHOSE THIS QUOTE:

> ## In all of the worlds, what is most wondrous? That no man, no woman, though they see people dying all around them, believes it will happen to them.

King Yudhisthira, Mahabharata, *Hindu epic poem*

THEME: EMBRACING DEATH

In our contemporary culture, we make an enormous effort to keep death at arm's length. We spend more than 50% of our health care dollars in the final six months of life, literally throwing money at death. We shut away our elders in nursing homes to avoid confronting their pain and our destiny. We have a multi-billion dollar cosmetics industry that tries to keep us all looking young. We even put rouge on people in the coffin.

The ancient spiritual traditions remind us to keep death as an advisor, because the recollection of our death can lend power, grace and fullness to every moment. *When we come into contact with precarious nature of this life, we also come to appreciate its preciousness. Then we don't want to waste a minute. Death shows us what is most important. We tell those we love that we love them. We enter our lives more fully.*

It is an absurd gamble to wait until the time of our death to learn the lessons that dying has to teach. To imagine that at the time of our death, we will have the physical strength, emotional stability and intellectual clarity to do the work of a lifetime is at best wishful thinking. We must learn now, live now and meet our fears now. Practice now.

MINDFULNESS PRACTICE FOR THE WEEK

Settle into the breath and body. Soften the heart.
Open the mind. Abide in the breath.

When the mind wanders away from this contemplation, notice how it turns to sleep or other thoughts, how it resists or avoids. Call it back to face the truth.

Gently repeat the phrases below from the Anguttara Nikaya Buddhist scriptures (5.57, The Five Reflections/Remembrances):

I am of the nature to grow old.
There is no way to escape growing old.

I am of the nature to have ill health.
There is no way to escape ill health.

I am of the nature to die.
There is no way to escape death.

All that is dear to me and everyone I love are of the nature to change.
There is no way to escape being separated from them.

My actions are my only true belongings.
I cannot escape the consequences of my actions.
My actions are the ground upon which I stand.

Section VII

Discovering Happiness & Joy

Mindfulness teaches a new discovery and appreciation of happiness and joy.

JACK KORNFIELD, Ph.D. CHOSE THIS QUOTE

"

Sun drapes a buttered scarf across your shoulder, Rose opens herself to your glance, Rain shares its divine melancholy, The whole world keeps nibbling your ear like a neglected lover.

"

Alison Luterman, Consider the Generosity of The One-Year-Old, *2002*

Yes, there is suffering in life, and our sorrows need to be met and tended with the great compassion of the heart. But suffering is not the end of the story.

There is also an unshakable joy that is possible for us as human beings. This is called the "happiness for no cause." It is a luminous reflection of our undying spirit. It is the smile of Nelson Mandela, the optimism of Aung San Suu Kyi and the laughter of the Dalai Lama. This can be your smile too.

The Buddha instructs us to cultivate our heart in this way: "Live in joy, in love, even among those who hate. Live in joy, to health, even among the afflicted. Live in joy and peace, even among the troubled."

{ MINDFULNESS PRACTICE FOR THE WEEK }

With a spirit of wise attention you can honor the vast gifts of beauty on this earth alongside your measure of sorrows. You will need some healing for your pains. But do not be overly loyal to your suffering. A peaceful heart and a vast perspective can be yours as well. Look up at the stars. See the oak trees and the tender evening light. Open your eyes and become a witness to the mystery of incarnation, with its 10,000 joys and 10,000 sorrows. Let your story move on. It is never too late. With a beginner's mind start again. Take a big breath. You are free to choose your spirit. Choose love. Dance.

RICHARD FIELDS, Ph.D. CHOSE THIS QUOTE:

66

All beings want to be happy, yet so very few know how. It is out of ignorance that any of us cause suffering for ourselves or for others.

99

Sharon Salzberg,
Loving-kindness: The Revolutionary Art of Happiness, *1997*

THEME – HAPPINESS & JOY ARE NOW HERE

We often see happiness and joy as something we will attain in the future. We think that when we have enough money, have the right job, have the right house, the right relationship, the right family situation, then we will be happy and joyful. We blind ourselves with this fantasy that we think will make us happy. In striving for future happiness, we lose sight of happiness and joy in the present situation.

For example, read the following jumble of words to yourself:

JOYISNOWHERE

Some people will read it as "Joy is nowhere." You can also read it as "Joy is now here."

No matter what the past or our hoped-for future, there is happiness and joy to be found if we open our eyes and our hearts to the present situation. Cultivating gratitude is a good way to recognize and affirm the happiness and joy in your life.

{ MINDFULNESS PRACTICE FOR THE WEEK }

Sit down in a quiet place and make a list of all the things that you are grateful for in your present situation.

Then pick one or two — or many — people for whom you are grateful.

Write a letter to each one, as many as you want, and thank them for being in your life and for the support they have given you.

Kiss each envelope, and mail your letters. Consider taking a quiet meditative walk to a mailbox or post office.

Repeat to yourself "Joy is now here. Joy is now here."

When you are feeling joyful or happy, affirm to yourself, "Joy is now here."

42

LARRY CAMMARATA, Ph.D. CHOSE THIS QUOTE:

Joy is being willing for things to be as they are.

Charlotte Joko Beck, Nothing Special, *1993*

This quote by the late American Zen teacher Charlotte Joko Beck captures the spirit of mindfulness in meditation and in everyday life situations. The power of this quote is its ability to cut through what separates us from the joy that is always with us.

When I contemplate the wisdom of these words, *I realize that joy is not something that I have to seek in order to find.* The joy of the present moment is always accessible through my willingness to accept and embrace reality on reality's terms.

Joy is a thread that integrates and unifies the fabric of our mind, body and relationships, a thread that is frequently broken by our judgments, stories, future plans and inattentiveness.

When we encounter our internal experiences and outer relationships directly, we experience the energy of raw, unadulterated contact with life, as it is, not how we wish it to be. *This direct connection to the energy of life can be called "joy," since it is uplifting and aligned with life, not against anyone or anything.*

Joy is like the clear blue sky. Our opinions and judgments are like clouds; although they can obscure the clarity of the sky, they are temporary and unsubstantial in nature. *When we identify with the clouds, we disconnect from the joy that is always there, behind the clouds. When we patiently accept the presence of the clouds without attributing truth to them, they will eventually pass, revealing the clarity of the blue sky.*

⟨ MINDFULNESS PRACTICE FOR THE WEEK ⟩

The practice of mindfulness allows us an opportunity to gently shine the light of open, nonjudgmental awareness upon our manipulation of the present moment.

In this moment, you are invited to let the clouds pass and experience the clarity also known as "joy" that is here for you, right now.

Section VIII

{ QUOTES № 43 TO 52 }

Interconnectedness
&
"Loving-kindness"

*Mindfulness reminds us how we are interconnected
and the importance of making connection
and expressing loving-kindness.*

43

Roshi Joan Halifax, Ph.D. chose this quote:

> **Whatever joy there is in this world
> All comes from desiring others to be happy,
> And whatever suffering there is in this world,
> All comes from desiring myself to be happy.**
>
> **But what need is there to say much more?
> The childish work for their own benefit,
> The Buddhas work for the benefit of others.**

Shantideva, Guide to the Bodhisattva's Life, *8th century*

THEME – HAVING EMPATHY

How wonderful, these words of Shantideva. And then we ask: how do we realize this joy? *I feel that one of the things that is really important to do in our life with others is to really sense what their experience is.* The practice that follows is about fostering empathy and taking perspective. It can be done alone or sitting in an airport, or walking on the beach, or being in a crowd at a meeting or class. *Just letting yourself feel the heart and mind of others opens the world in a very special way.*

To begin, please bring your mind and heart to the presence of someone who is having a difficult time — maybe a friend or relative, someone you feel close to.

Open your heart and mind to this person. Really let yourself sense his or her situation. Feel your way into this person's heart.
(Pause)

What are they going through? What is their experience?
(Pause)

Now let yourself imagine looking out through their eyes.
(Long pause)

Imagine that you are this person, living his or her life, feeling his or her suffering, knowing his or her heart.
(Long pause)

Feel how this friend, this relative, experiences the world, experiences life.

Now imagine that you are this other person, looking out through their eyes, feeling into their experience, seeing how they might see the world, sensing how they experience their body. Imagine that you have been through what they have been through.

Exchange yourself for them, live in their body for a few moments, as you look out through their eyes.
(Long pause)

Now gently shift your attention back to your breath. Stay with the breath for the next moments.
(Long pause)

Completing your practice, please offer this person whatever good has arisen for you in this session.

Wish the best for him or her, saying to yourself:
May you find peace and well-being....
(Pause)

Let that sense of tenderness, kindness and goodness flow from you to him or her.
(Pause)

Throughout the day, remind yourself to bring the spirit of this practice into your everyday life in order to benefit others and yourself.

44

ELISHA GOLDSTEIN, Ph.D. CHOSE THIS QUOTE:

"

The biggest disease today is not leprosy or tuberculosis but rather the feeling of not belonging.

"

Mother Teresa

THEME – MAKING CONNECTION & BELONGING

Mother Teresa saw too many people who were ostracized by society; she knew better than most the pain of not belonging. That pain lives in our culture.

One of the aims of the national research study I conducted in 2005 was to distill down the essence of feeling well. I discovered that the word people used more than any other to describe their experience of well-being was "connection."

As human beings, we are wired toward connection. In order to feel healthy, we need to feel a sense of community, a sense that we belong and are not alone. The problem is our culture makes it very difficult to belong from the start.

From the time when we are young, we are sent the message that we need to look a certain way or act a certain way in order to "fit in." We try to conform because, in our culture, we often don't accept those who are different. *In fact, history shows us that we fear those people who are different and often are quick to judge, isolate and even oppress them.*

So imagine that if belonging is so important to our health and well-being and we are a culture that is quick to cast out those who are different, it is easy for a deep-seeded fear to be planted in each of us from a very young age that perhaps we won't belong and that this would be intolerable. When we perceive that we don't belong, we look for ways to escape this intolerable feeling. These attempts to escape might include falling into a numb, depressed state; becoming anxious; or resorting to drugs, alcohol or other addictive behaviors.

Just think for a second: was there ever a time you didn't feel like you belonged or felt ostracized? What was your experience? What were you thinking and feeling?

We thrive when we feel connection.

Psychologist Dr. Gary Schwartz has a handy model that says, *"Awareness leads to connection which leads to balance; unawareness leads to disconnection, which leads to imbalance."* In other words, when we begin to cultivate an awareness of our thoughts, feelings and emotions, we become connected to them, which helps us become more balanced. When we are unaware of them or on auto-pilot, we are disconnected from them, and it is much more likely that they will take us over in fits of anxiety, anger or depression.

So connection can begin with us. We can begin by bringing mindful awareness to our thoughts, feelings and/or emotions. Even just a few minutes of non-judgmental awareness of our feelings in any moment can be a moment of connection, balance and healing.

⎰ Mindfulness Practice for the Week ⎱

If you're feeling sadness, notice that sadness and bring a kind attention to where you feel that in the body, exploring it with a sense of curiosity and even imagining yourself holding this pain in your arms like you would imagine the archetypal nurturing mother figure doing (even though most of us did not have this, we might be able to imagine it).
Just do this for a few minutes at a time and see what happens.

Always thank yourself for taking the time to do this.
Time is precious and so giving time toward this is a gift, and that is why we try and send gratitude inwards.

45

SHARON SALZBERG CHOSE THIS QUOTE:

66

Abandon what is unskillful. One can abandon the unskillful. If it were not possible, I would not ask you to do so.

99

The Buddha

THEME – LIVING CONSCIOUSLY

This is one of my favorite passages from the Buddha's teaching. I think it beautifully exemplifies his extraordinary compassion. The mind of the Buddha doesn't see good and bad people, but sees life's suffering and the potential of the end of suffering. *Rather than condemning them, the Buddha exhorts those heading directly toward suffering through greed or anger or fear to take care, to pay attention, to see how much more they are capable of.*

This is a passage that inspires a feeling of great self-confidence — it can be done.... I can do it. Even I can do it. Otherwise the Buddha would not have asked me to do so.

What the Buddha is encouraging isn't a state of arrogance or conceit or excessive pride. He is talking about a state of *heartful courage.* The realization that we are capable of so much is essential to our flourishing as full human beings. This calling forth of confident effort is the offering of personal empowerment, of faith in ourselves. *We can make changes in our lives, we can live consciously rather than mechanically, we can open our hearts and we can be more fully alive. If it were not possible, the Buddha wouldn't ask us to do it.*

┤ MINDFULNESS PRACTICE FOR THE WEEK ├

*Sit quietly and call to mind an endeavor you are involved with —
a project, a shift in a relationship, a communication you are about
to have. See if you can discern what your aspiration is — what do
you hope for, what is your dream, what would reveal the fruit
of your efforts as successful? If you find that aspiration, rest with it
a moment, then see if you can make it bigger, more daring,
more expansive. If you are trying to stop smoking, for example,
maybe expand that to dealing with stress in a better way.
If you want to feel powerful, are you willing to explore different
measures of strength and not be limited to a conventional picture of power?*
Be mindful of what it feels like as you expand your field of aspiration.

46

JENNY PHILLIPS, Ph.D. CHOSE THIS QUOTE:

"

No man is an island entire of itself;
every man is a piece of the
continent, a part of the main.
If a clod be washed away by the sea,
Europe is the less, as well as if a
promontory were, as well as if
a manor of thy friend's or of thine
own were: any man's death diminishes
me, because I am involved in mankind,
and therefore never send to know for
whom the bell tolls; it tolls for thee.

"

John Donne,
Meditation XVII, Devotions Upon Emergent Occasions *(1624)*

The beauty of these words by John Donne, poet and priest, jolt me out of the mindless preoccupations of daily life. Perhaps it is because the words of the 17th-century metaphysical poet are timeless and lyrical. They conjure an image of a piece of earth dropping into the sea and ceasing to exist, a small event that diminishes a massive solid continent.

When Ernest Hemingway chose *For Whom the Bell Tolls* as a title for one of his books, he worried that people might "think only of tolls as long distance charges or of Bell as the Bell telephone system." He nevertheless concluded, "I think it has the magic that a title has to have."

Hemingway's worry that the title might not be fully grasped and, instead, be interpreted in a limited, materialistic way, is posed for me by the haunting power of Donne's words. *Can we experience this interconnectedness among all mankind, or will it be lost in the insignificances of daily life? That is the question.*

{ MINDFULNESS PRACTICE FOR THE WEEK }

Sit in a comfortable position. Let your mind be still.
Focus on the breath as you repeat phrases of
"loving-kindness" over and over.

May all beings be filled with loving-kindness.
May all beings be well.
May all beings be peaceful and at ease.
May all beings be happy.

Hold an image or sense the presence of all those to whom
you are sending selfless love and good wishes. Feel the Metta
coming from your heart and moving forth into the universe.

WILLIAM MORGAN, PSY.D. CHOSE THIS QUOTE:

66

When an enemy arises in your life, even though you may kill it, another will simply arise, because all arisings are simply a manifestation of your own state of consciousness.

99

Kalu Rinpoche, 20th-century Buddhist monk and teacher

THEME – TURNING AWAY FROM ENEMIES

The Buddha highlighted a central aspect of our self-created dissatisfaction. In our efforts to be happy, we excessively orchestrate the moment by avoiding, rejecting or disowning certain aspects of our experience. While this may be temporarily effective, it establishes a duality where some things are acceptable and others not. Since an alternation between pleasant and unpleasant thoughts, feelings and perceptions is inevitable, this approach cannot lead to a deeper sense of freedom and contentment.

In addition, the very habit of turning away from "enemies" has become well established yet unexamined. At some point, we need to open up to what was previously unacceptable or intolerable. In theory, this will happen naturally and organically in the course of meditation practice, but we are deeply wired to avoid unpleasant experience. It may therefore be helpful to bring direct attention to this deeply engrained tendency through the following exercise.

{ MINDFULNESS PRACTICE FOR THE WEEK }

■

Establish a relaxed posture and easy breath.

■

While maintaining this relaxed state, slowly bring to mind a moderately uncomfortable memory, allowing an initial flow of images to arise for just a few seconds.

■

Notice the aversion arising in the mind and the tension in the body.

■

Let go of the memory and reestablish relaxation in your body and breath.

■

Bring the memory to mind once again, consciously trying to stay relaxed as you do so.

■

Continue to alternate between these states until it is possible to stay relaxed while holding the unpleasant memory in your mind.

The freedom we are aiming for involves changing our relationship to the present moment, and this happens not through excessive orchestrating, but by creating a holding environment for the full range of our human experience

48

KAREN KISSEL WEGELA, Ph.D. CHOSE THIS QUOTE:

"

May I be a bridge.

"

Shantideva, Guide to the Bodhisattva's Way of Life, *8th Century*

THEME – HELPING OTHERS – BEING OF SERVICE

This quote from Shantideva points to one of the most powerful benefits of practicing mindfulness: the increased ability to be of service to others. In the passage from which this quote comes, Shantideva aspires to be whatever is needed to help other beings who are suffering: a bridge, a boat, a doctor – whatever it takes. I have always been moved by his compassion, and I particularly like the image of being a bridge, a connection. Since I work as a teacher and as a therapist, I am often trying to be a kind of bridge to help my students and clients connect with their own inner wisdom, with others in their lives and with their own aspirations to benefit others. Often, it is simply the human connection of being together with another that provides a sense of healing for us.

Mindfulness makes our bodily sensations, emotions, thoughts and images more vivid. As we become more fully present in our lives, we become increasingly aware of our own pain and the pain of others. We naturally want to reach out to them and long to relieve their suffering. It may mean something simple like offering a sad friend a cup of tea. It might mean volunteering in a homeless shelter. Or it could mean sitting with a relative or friend who is sick or dying. In all those situations, we may be a bridge, a way of connecting with others who may be feeling alone and possibly frightened in their suffering.

With increased mindfulness, we not only notice our desire to help others, we are actually more able to do so. We are more present and able to see what might be useful.

In my life, I have made it a practice to ask myself,
"How may I be a bridge in this situation?"
How can I bring my mindfulness and my tender heart
to bear in a way that helps myself and others?

During this week, you can practice in this way, too.
Begin by contemplating, thinking about, what being a bridge
might mean for you. Feel free to change the metaphor
to something that works better for you if you like. Then, as a
mindfulness practice, simply notice when you feel the desire
to be of service or to alleviate the pain of another.
Use your mindfulness just to notice your experience,
not to judge what you find. You may notice a desire to
help those you know well. You may feel a pain in your
heart when you witness the confusion or frustration of a loved one.
Or you may notice that you never feel moved in that way at all.
Whatever you notice is fine. Just continue the practice
and see what, if anything, shifts over the course of the week.
If you have trouble remembering to notice these feelings,
you can build in specific times to check in with yourself —
maybe first thing in the morning or at the end of the day
before going to bed. Over time, if you feel like you'd like to
continue this practice, you may notice that it becomes easier
to track the natural inclination to be of service.
Of course, if you choose to actually do or say something
to benefit another, that's fine, too!

49

AMY WEINTRAUB, MFA, ERYT-500 CHOSE THIS QUOTE:

" In the breath, the soul finds an opportunity to speak. "

Danna Faulds, "Breath," Go In and In, *2002*

THEME – SYNCHRONIZING BREATH & INTERCONNECTEDNESS

I know of no better way to sense our interconnectedness than to begin a breathing practice. Aside from the well-documented health benefits, we can stop a ruminative chain of thoughts or a negative mood state in its tracks with *one of many simple yogic breathing exercises called pranayama.* Trauma, loss and the everyday hassles of daily life can create constriction in the physical and emotional body. As we constrict, we begin to close off from others. Some of us carry this sense of separation throughout our lives in the form of depression.

Yogic breathing can begin to break through that wall of separation, perhaps just a chink at first, through which we begin to feel less separate and alone. A simple breath can give us a felt sense of our connection to the energy of the cosmos.

Einstein once said that we are operating under the optical delusion of our separateness and that our separateness is lethal. *When we breathe mindfully, that delusion dissolves and we begin to see clearly again that we are intimately and eternally connected to the energy of the universe and to each other. What is authentic within us is given voice.*

OCEAN-SOUNDING VICTORY BREATH (UJJAYI)

*When we breathe consciously, we may quiet the clatter
of thoughts so that mindfulness naturally arises. Try this simple
breath when the busy mind needs a respite. Let it be the
portal into your seated meditation practice.*

*This breath, jokingly referred to as Darth Vader Breath,
is soothing to the central nervous system, even as it calms
the mind and supports greater focus for meditation.*

■

*Inhale through the nostrils to the count of four with a
slight constriction at the back of the throat, so that the
breath is audible, like a light snoring sound.*

■

*Exhale through the nostrils for four counts,
maintaining the snoring sound.*

■

*The breath is slow and deep. Feel the breath expanding
the belly, the rib cage and then the upper chest.*

■

*On the exhalation, pull the abdomen in
and up to empty the lungs completely.*

■

Sense the breath at the back of the throat.

■

*Listen to your breath. Does it sound like a wave gently
rolling across pebbles? Imagine your favorite pebbly beach.
Does it sound like an infant's snore? Let it be like a
lullaby to yourself — perhaps a younger you....*

Cool, isn't it ?

50

Stan Tatkin, Psy.D., MFT chose this quote:

66

The most precious gift we can offer others is our presence. When mindfulness embraces those we love, they will bloom like flowers.

99

Thich Nhat Hanh, Vietnamese Buddhist Monk

THEME – BEING PRESENT IN INTIMATE PARTNER RELATIONSHIPS

While mindfulness is an exquisitely simple means for attending to and accepting our moment-by-moment experience, I believe it can also be a gateway for improving intimate experiences with another person.

The use of mutual gaze and of the face as an object of meditation, along with an attitude of allowingness, seems to invite the experience Thich Nhat Hanh describes.

I am a couples therapist, and whenever I see couples interact as Thich Nhat Hanh describes, the partners seem to "bloom as flowers" as each closely attends to the other's face, eyes, voice and body. I find a similar experience as I closely attend to my clients' expressions, gestures and movements. My body remains relaxed and my mind alert as I follow the continuous shifting of sensations, thought and feeling — both within my body and those of the couple. *Our total experience of another person is amplified when we closely watch his or her face while preserving our own equanimity.*

Admittedly, I am biased as a therapist who loves to read faces and places a high value on positive interactions between partners.

{ MINDFULNESS PRACTICE FOR THE WEEK }

I recommend couples gaze into each other's eyes as either a bedtime or morning mindfulness meditation practice. First, silently note any body sensations as they arise and fade (e.g., "legs... foot... head... chest... head").

If thoughts or urges become intrusive, include those as well (e.g., "judging... judging... urge... head... chest... urge... memory...").

After using your own body sensations or thoughts as the object of meditation, switch to using your partner's face as the object.

Notice any and all changes that sweep across the neck, face and eyes.
Both partners can silently note "change...change...same...change" or "expanding...contracting" if they are able to do so. The noting can also be performed as a quiet tapping on your own leg, as long as it isn't obvious to your partner.

This is not only a good mindfulness exercise for partner connection, but also serves as a real-time tracking of each other's autonomic nervous system. Gazing has both stimulating and calming properties and leads naturally to loving feelings. As a bonus, mindfulness practice done this way builds mutual parasympathetic tone and often leads to sensual activities following the meditation.

The first part of the exercise builds self-regulatory skills, while the second addresses interactive regulatory skills. Partners can discuss and compare their experiences when they have completed the practice. I believe this is a winning mindfulness practice for anyone who is coupled!

51

M. Kathleen B. Lustyk, Ph.D. chose this quote:

66

If we have no peace, it is because we have forgotten that we belong to each other.

99

Mother Teresa

THEME – DEVELOPING PEACE AND INTERCONNECTEDNESS

This quote is printed on a decorative banner that I have hanging in my office, a gift from someone who knows that I research stress. They thought I would enjoy the simplicity of the message. I enjoy the banner very much and I often find myself reflecting on its message.

While the message may be simple, cultivating an appreciation for interconnectedness and a love for all beings is far from effortless.

Mother Teresa's words are a testament to her Christian philosophy, according to which we are all God's children. Said another way, we are all brothers and sisters in Christ. *The Buddha also taught of our interconnectedness and said that the path to end suffering and acquire true peace requires embodying loving-kindness.*

The Buddha taught how to cultivate loving-kindness through a practice of approaching what we fear with love. As the story goes, a group of monks and nuns went into the jungle to practice being aware of their bodies and minds as instructed by the Buddha. However, after nightfall the jungle grew dark and frightening, making it too difficult for them to practice their meditation. So the Buddha offered them a practice that would keep them from fear: the loving-kindness meditation. This practice awakens the nobility of the heart so that living with loving intention becomes our very nature. This practice allowed the monks to wish well all of the creatures in the jungle, including those they feared.

The simple fact is that all of us at times find ourselves caught up in fear or anger. As with those of the monks in the forest, our own fears or other strong negative emotions can render us incapable of engaging in behaviors we enjoy, and cause us to suffer. *The Buddha taught a practice that allows us to experience love, not fear, thus reducing Dukkha or suffering. Mother Teresa also taught the importance of love, believing that with love all things are possible, including peace.*

────────────┤ MINDFULNESS PRACTICE FOR THE WEEK ├────────────

So how does one practice loving-kindness meditation?
There are many verses, found throughout this book, that one can use.
But the following one, designed to cultivate peace in oneself, is in keeping
with the message of Mother Teresa and the theme offered here.

Begin by assuming the meditation posture that is comfortable
for you and take a few deep breaths letting go of tension.
Next, repeat the following phrases to yourself:

■

May I (you) be free from fear and anger.

■

May I (you) be free from danger.

■

May I (you) be peaceful and happy.

■

May I (you) be at ease in my (your) body and mind.

■

May my (your) love for myself (yourself) flow boundlessly.

I like to repeat one of these phrases a few times before moving on to the next one. Next, bring to mind a person for whom you have felt anger and who has been angry with you. You may notice that the tension has returned to you body. Take a few deep breaths and try to let go of that tension. Then, recite the phrases, replacing the word I with you, while holding the image of this difficult person in your mind's eye. I like to envision the person smiling, healthy and with a strong body, and getting embraced in the way a loving mother holds their baby, bestowing unconditional love, security and safety on them.

I find the latter image helps especially when I offer up my meditation to a person who has hurt me or for a person with whom I find particularly difficult to work. In those instances where it's hard for me to bring my own feelings of love to the person, I find I can get there through the model offered by the loving mother. This is not easy and the practitioner should be prepared to invest himself or herself in this practice. But it's worth it. When we replace feelings of anger and fear with love and compassion, we are the ones who suffer less. We are the ones who are left feeling peaceful. Once again we see the theme present in all of the teachings offered in this book: We get to experience what we practice for ourselves.
If we play over thoughts of anger, we feel stress.
If we play over thoughts of love and compassion,
we feel peaceful. The choice is ours.

SYLVIA BOORSTEIN, Ph.D., LCSW CHOSE THIS QUOTE:

"

May all beings, omitting none, feel safe and content and happy, and live with ease.

"

Metta Sutta

THEME – SEEING OTHERS

"I see you," is the phrase that the humanoid beings in the film *Avatar* use to mean *"I deeply understand who you are and I feel connected to you unreservedly."* It has been my experience from the start of my career as a psychologist that therapists practicing across the spectrum of therapies agree that the essential healing element in all therapeutic collaborations is the sense of being truly seen. I'm beginning to think that even more healing than the sense of being seen is the conviction that someone wants to see us and is willing to suspend preconceived ideas, views and opinions in order to do that.

I find that I am easily moved by the situations of people I don't recognize. On an overnight coast-to-coast flight, I feel compassion for the people around me scrunched into apparently uncomfortable positions. I wish them (and myself) a safe end to the journey. I feel we are fellow-travelers, keeping each other company. At the opera, I feel delighted for the people around me shouting "bravo" and clapping in a standing ovation. *I'm sure they are as thrilled as I am and I know their presence has heightened my own pleasure.*

If, however, as I walk down the cabin aisle of the red-eye flight I recognize a person toward whom I feel antipathy — a colleague who has criticized me, a former friend who has disappointed me — the startle of the moment erases both my generalized compassion for the whole planeload of people and the pleasure I had when I felt it. If, when the lights come up in the opera, the person next to me is wearing a button with a political slogan on it that I disagree with, I feel my mind wobble in hesitation before saying to that person, "That was great, wasn't it?"

Seeing people as people just like myself, without pre-conditioning stories, allows me to remember that everyone suffers and delights just as I do in this ever-challenging life and evokes in me empathic responses of compassion or joy that do not depend on particulars. I would like to be able to wish, as the Metta Sutta instructs, "May all beings, omitting none, feel safe, and content, and happy, and live with ease." To the extent that I can "see" others on this intimate level, I will feel supported by my own natural benevolence.

The planet where *Avatar* unfolds is a place of peace. I think the message of the film is that living in a world supported by peace, where people "see" each other truly as kin with whom it is safe to connect, is an expression of hope for human beings. We haven't, as a species, gotten there yet, but maybe we will. *We are wired, I believe, for compassion, so I am hopeful that we can achieve that connection.*

{ LAST MINDFULNESS PRACTICE }

*"May all beings omitting none, feel safe, and content,
and happy, and live with ease."*

Metta Sutta

Appendix

.

Contributors

.

Photo Credits

.

EDITOR, CONTRIBUTING AUTHOR

RICHARD FIELDS, Ph.D.

Richard is the founder/director of FACES Conferences, Inc. (www.facesconferences.com), and trainer/creator of the workshop *Quieting the Hungry Ghost: Mindulness & Relapse Prevention*. For over thirty years he had an outpatient private counseling practice, specializing in alcohol/drug recovery and relapse prevention.

He is the author of the college textbook *Drugs in Perspective*, 8th edition, McGraw-Hill, 2012, and *Awakening to Mindfulness*, HCI, 2008. He is dedicated to bringing mindfulness to the world.

CONTRIBUTING TEACHERS

MELISSA MYOZEN BLACKER ROSHI

Melissa is a Zen teacher, priest, and co-founder and abbot of Boundless Way Zen. She is in residence at Boundless Way Temple in Worcester, MA. She was a teacher and director of programs at the Center for Mindfulness at the University of Massachusetts Medical School for 19 years, and now has a private practice in spiritual direction and mindfulness consulting. (www.melissablacker.com)

Melissa is co-editor of *The Book of Mu: Essential Writings on Zen's Most Important Koan*, and her writing appears in *Best Buddhist Writing*, 2012.

SYLVIA BOORSTEIN, Ph.D., LCSW

Sylvia is Cofounding teacher of Spirit Rock Meditation Center. She is the author of five books on Buddhism, mindfulness, and meditation. Her most recent book is *Happiness Is An Inside Job: Practicing for a Joyful Life.*

Sylvia has four adult children and seven grandchildren.

TARA BRACH, Ph.D.

Tara is founder and senior teacher of the Insight Meditation Community of Washington, D.C. and teaches Buddhist meditation at centers in the United States and Canada. A clinical psychologist, she has taught extensively on the application of Buddhist teachings to emotional healing. Dr. Brach is the author of *Radical Acceptance: Embracing Your Life with the Heart of a Buddha* (Bantam, 2002) and the upcoming book *True Refuge: Finding Peace and Freedom in Your Own Awakened Heart* (Bantam, 2013). For Tara's teaching schedule, free talks and guided meditations, please visit Tarabrach.com.

JOHN BRIERE, Ph.D.

John is Associate Professor of Psychiatry at the University of Southern California and Director of the Psychological Trauma Program at LAC+USC Medical Center, where he teaches and consults in the emergency room, psychiatric hospital, and burn unit. He is the recipient of the American Psychological Association's Award for Outstanding Contributions to the Science of Trauma Psychology. He is the author of various articles, chapters, and books on trauma, posttraumatic stress, and mindfulness. His website is www.johnbriere.com.

LARRY CAMMARATA, Ph.D.

Larry is a Clinical Psychologist specializing in mind-body medicine and is the Clinical Director of Skyland Behavioral Health Associates in Asheville, NC.

He regularly conducts qigong workshops at FACES Conferences. He is the author of the DVD, *Qigong for Health and Vitality: The Eight Pieces of Brocade*

CHRISTOPHER GERMER, Ph.D.

Chris is a clinical instructor in Psychology at Harvard Medical School. He is the author of *The Mindful Path to Self-Compassion* and co-editor of *Wisdom and Compassion in Psychotherapy*, and *Mindfulness and Psychotherapy*

ELISHA GOLDSTEIN, Ph.D.

Elisha is a Psychologist, Educator, and author of *The Now Effect: How this Moment can Change the rest of your Life.*

He is also the co-author of *The Mindfulness-Based Stress Reduction Workbook*. He has a private psychotherapy practice in West Los Angeles, California, and can be contacted at www.elishagoldstein.com.

ROSHI JOAN HALIFAX, Ph.D.

Roshi Joan is a Buddhist teacher, anthropologist, author and social activist. She is the Abbott and head teacher at Upaya Zen Center in Santa Fe, N.M. She is the author of many books including *Being with Dying.*

Rick Hanson, Ph.D.

Rick is a neuropsychologist and author of *Buddha's Brain*,
He is the founder of Wellspring Institute for Neuroscience
and Contemplative Wisdom, and Affiliate of the Greater
Good Science Center at UC Berkeley.

Steven C. Hayes, Ph.D.

Steve is a professor of psychology at the University of Nevada,
Reno, and a developer of Acceptance and Commitment
Therapy (ACT) and Relational Frame Theory (RFT). The
latter is a basic research program on human language and
cognition that has among other things developed the data
on the cognitive basis of perspective taking mentioned in his
commentary. His best-known popular book is *Get Out of Your
Mind and Into Your Life* (with Spencer Smith, 2005). To find out
more about ACT and RFT, go to www.contextualpsychology.org,
the site of the Association for Contextual Behavioral Science.

Susan Kaiser-Greenland, JD

Susan is the author of *The Mindful Child* (Free Press, 2010)
and a former corporate attorney. Susan developed the
Inner Kids program for children, teens and their families
and teaches worldwide.

Jack Kornfield, Ph.D.

Jack is an internationally renowned meditation teacher, and
one of the leaders in introducing Buddhist practice and
psychology to the West.

Trained as a Buddhist monk in Thailand, Burma, and India.
Jack is an inspiring master teacher. He is the founder and
director Spirit Rock Center in northern California. He is
the author of many books including *A Path With Heart*, and
The Wise Heart.

Gregg Krech

Gregg is a leading expert in Japanese Psychology and the
author of several books including *Naikan: Gratitude, Grace, and
the Japanese Art of Self-Reflection*, and *A Natural Approach to Mental
Wellness*. He is the Director of the ToDo Institute in Vermont –
an educational and retreat center (www.todoinstitute.org).
His blog is at www.thirtythousanddays.org

Roshi Marsha Linehan, Ph.D.

Professor of Psychology, Director of the Behavioral Research & Therapy Clinics, University of Washington, and author of *Cognitive-Behavioral Treatment of Borderline Personality Disorder*.

Dr. Linehan has translated aspects of both Zen and Contemplative practices into behaviorally specific instructions for mindfulness practice that can be taught to clients in psychotherapy. She has been a Zen Teacher under Jaeger Roshi since 2004 and a Zen Teacher in the Diamond Sangha since 2009. Linehan@uw.edu

M. Kathleen B. Lustyk, Ph.D.

Kathy is a Professor of Psychology at Seattle Pacific University. In addition to teaching Behavioral Neuroscience and Women's Health courses, she is the Primary Investigator of the Women's Health Lab (http:www.spu.edu/LustykLab).

Kathy also holds affiliate faculty positions in the School of Nursing and Department of Psychology at the University of Washington, where she engages in research on the effects of Mindfulness-Based Relapse Prevention on addictive behaviors in women.

Michael Meade, D.H.L.

Michael is a renowned storyteller, author and scholar of mythology, anthropology, and psychology. He combines hypnotic and fiery storytelling, street savvy perceptiveness, and spellbinding interpretations of ancient myths with a deep knowledge of cross cultural rituals.

Michael is the founder of Mosaic Multicultural Foundation, author of *Fate and Destiny, The World Behind the World*, and *The Water of Life*. For more information, about Mosaic and Michael, visit www.mosaicvoices.org.

Phillip Moffitt

Phillip is Co-Guiding Teacher at Spirit Rock Meditation Center in Woodacre, California and Founder of Life Balance Institute. He is the author of *Emotional Chaos to Clarity: How to Live More Skillfully, Make Better Decisions, and Find Purpose in Life* (Penguin, 2012) and *Dancing with Life: Buddhist Insights for Finding Meaning and Joy in the Face of Suffering* (Rodale, 2008). To find out more about Phillip and his teachings and work, go to www.dharmawisdom.org and www.lifebalance.org.

WILLIAM MORGAN, Psy.D.
Bill Morgan, is a founding board member of the
Institute for Meditation and Psychotherapy in Boston
(meditationandpsychotherapy.org). He is a contributor to
Mindfulness and Psychotherapy. Bill has participated in more
than 6 years of silent meditation retreats in the Theravadan,
Zen, and Tibetan traditions, and has also spent 6 months
in a Trappist monastery. Bill teaches retreats for mental
health professionals, and has recently completed 2½ years
of intensive retreat.

RUBIN NAIMAN, Ph.D.
Rubin is a psychologist, clinical assistant professor of medicine
and the sleep and dream specialist at the University of Arizona's
Center for Integrative Medicine, directed by Dr. Andrew Weil.
He maintains a private practice in Tucson, AZ, and provides
consultation and training. He is the author of a number of
works on sleep, including *Healing Night, Healthy Sleep* (with Dr.
Weil), and *The Yoga of Sleep*.

KRISTIN NEFF, Ph.D.
Kristin is an Associate Professor of Human Development
and Culture at the Educational Psychology Dept. of the
University of Texas at Austin She is a pioneer in the field
of self-compassion research and author of *Self-Compassion*
(William Morrow, 2011)

Kristin is also featured in the best selling book and award-
winning documentary, *The Horse Boy*, which chronicles her
family's adventure with her son's autism.

FRANK OSTASESKI
Frank is a Buddhist teacher, founder of the Metta Institute and
co-founder of Zen Hospice Project, the first Buddhist hospice in
America. He is one of America's leading voices in contemplative
care of the dying. He can be reached at www.mettainstitute.org

JENNY PHILLIPS, Ph.D., MSN
Jenny is an author, filmmaker, cultural anthropologist, and
psychiatric nurse. She has a private practice in Concord, MA.
She is the author of *Letters From the Dhamma Brothers: Meditation
Behind Bars* and the producer and director of the award winning
documentary film *The Dhamma Brothers*. www.dhammabrothers.com;
jennyphillips101@aol.com

SHARON SALZBERG

Sharon is one of America's leading meditation teachers and writers. Her most recent book, *Real Happiness*, is a N.Y. Times Bestseller. She is also author of *The Kindness Handbook*, and *Loving-kindness: The Revolutionary Art of Happiness*.

SHAUNA L. SHAPIRO, Ph.D.

Shauna is an Associate Professor of Counseling Psychology at Santa Clara University, licensed clinical psychologist, and internationally recognized expert in the integration of mindfulness into Western psychology. She has conducted extensive clinical research investigating the effects of mindfulness training across a wide range of populations and has published over 70 peer-reviewed journal articles and book chapters in addition to co-authoring the text, *The Art and Science of Mindfulness*.

DANIEL J. SIEGEL, M.D.

Dan is the Executive Director of Mindsight Institute. He is a Clinical Professor of Psychiatry at the UCLA School of Medicine, and Co-Director of the UCLA Mindul Awareness Research Center.

He is the author of *The Developing Mind; Pocket Guide to Interpersonal Neurobiology*; *The Mindful Therapist; Mindsight*; and *The Mindful Brain*. He is co-author of *Parenting from the Inside Out* (with Mary Hartzell), and of *The Whole-Brain Child* (with Tina Bryson).

RONALD D. SIEGEL, Psy.D.

Ron is Assistant Clinical Professor of Psychology, Harvard Medical School and serves on the Board of Directors and faculty of the Institute for Meditation and Psychotherapy. He is the author of *The Mindfulness Solution: Everyday Practices for Everyday Problems*, co-editor of *Mindfulness and Psychotherapy*, and co-editor of *Wisdom and Compassion in Psychotherapy: Deepening Mindfulness in Clinical Practice*.

STAN TATKIN, Psy.D., MFT

Stan is a clinician, researcher, teacher, and developer of a Psychobiological Approach to Couple Therapy (PACT). He has a clinical practice in Calabasas, CA and is the author of *Wired for Love: How Understanding Your Partner's Brain and Attachment Style Can Help You Defuse Conflict and Build a Secure Relationship*.

Stan has developed a program to train other psychotherapists to use PACT in their clinical practice.

Karen Kissel Wegela, Ph.D.
Karen is the author of *The Courage to Be Present: Buddhism, Psychotherapy, and the Awakening of Natural Wisdom* (2009) and *What Really Helps: Using Mindfulness and Compassionate Presence to Help, Support, and Encourage Others* (2011), both from Shambhala. She is a professor in the M.A. Contemplative Psychotherapy program at Naropa University in Boulder and a psychologist in private practice.

Amy Weintraub, MFA, ERYT-500
Amy is the founder and director of LifeForce Yoga Healing Institute. She is the author of *Yoga for Depression* (Broadway books, 2004) and *Yoga Skills for Therapists: Effective Practices for Mood Management* (W.W. Norton, 2012), yogafordepression.com.

Polly Young-Eisendrath, Ph.D.
Polly is a Jungian analyst and psychologist in private practice in Central Vermont. She has published many books and chapters and her most recent is *The Self-Esteem Trap: Raising Confident and Compassionate Kids in an Age of Self-Importance.* She is working on a book on mindful love. Polly is also a certified mindfulness facilitator in the Vipassana tradition of Shinzen Young. www.young-eisendrath.com

{ PHOTO CREDITS }

COVER	|	*Vadim Ponomarenko*
PAGE 9	|	*Steven Frame*
PAGE 18	|	*Steven Frame*
PAGE 21	|	*Lisa Bradshaw*
PAGE 22	|	*Lisa Bradshaw*
PAGE 31	|	*Christoph Riddle*
PAGE 32	|	*Lisa Bradshaw*
PAGE 36	|	*Satori13*
PAGE 42	|	*Christoph Riddle*
PAGE 45	|	*Jacek Sajdak*
PAGE 48	|	*Lisa Bradshaw*
PAGE 59	|	*Jacek Sajdak*
PAGE 65	|	*Lisa Bradshaw*
PAGE 66	|	*Vadim Ponomarenko*
PAGE 70	|	*Madartists*
PAGE 72	|	*Abdullah Sm*
PAGE 78	|	*Lisa Bradshaw*
PAGE 91	|	*Lisa Bradshaw*
PAGE 97	|	*Lisa Bradshaw*
PAGE 105	|	*Lisa Bradshaw*
PAGE 110	|	*Lisa Bradshaw*
PAGE 113	|	*Jasenka*
PAGE 133	|	*Jasenka*